D1630576

No, Prime Minister!
Ralph Harris
Against the Consensus

A selection of the shorter writings of Ralph Harris
on the occasion of his 70th birthday

Institute of Economic Affairs
1994

First published in December 1994

by

THE INSTITUTE OF ECONOMIC AFFAIRS

2 Lord North Street, Westminster, London SW1P 3LB

Occasional Paper 94

ISSN 0073-909X

ISBN 0-255 36341-9

Cover design by David Lucas

Printed in Great Britain by

GORON PRO-PRINT CO LTD, LANCING, WEST SUSSEX

Set in Berthold Plantin 11 on 13 point

Contents

Foreword

WRITING short articles in newspapers and elsewhere is an extremely effective way of communicating ideas to a large and influential audience — provided the author has the gift of wit to catch his audience's attention, and the ability to make complex ideas simple. Ralph Harris, once a leader writer on *The Glasgow Herald*, has that gift and that ability. To celebrate his seventieth birthday in December 1994 and as a tribute to the exceptional influence which he has had on the intellectual climate in Britain and around the world, the Institute of Economic Affairs has assembled this selection from his hundreds of short articles.

Selection was a difficult task. We have tried, using thirty articles, to set out a representative collection of his thoughts. There was, at least, no doubt with which piece this tribute to him should begin. In 1975 he wrote an article which he called 'Cheer up! Things are getting worse' which, he tells friends, is his favourite among all his short pieces.

The article begins with a neat nine-paragraph summary of British post-war economic history, complete with character sketches of the leading politicians — that 'clever man Harold Wilson', 'dynamic George Brown', 'that nice Tony Barber', 'tough Ted', 'that smart Peter Walker' *et al.* As a result of their efforts, in 1975

> 'The welfare state is a seething mass of grievances, nationalised industries brought to the verge of insolvency, public spending above 55 per cent of GNP, the pound going under for the third time, foreign debts mortgaging our future, unemployment mounting towards one million, inflation roaring above 20 per cent and national bankruptcy staring us in the face.'

But what does national bankruptcy mean? — certainly not exhaustion of the skills and resources of the British people which '. . . have survived the assault and battery of government mismanagement'. The blame lies squarely with government, with the politicians and civil servants who have pretended they could solve Britain's economic problems.

v

'What is being bankrupted before your eyes is the post-war, all-party mythology that bigger and bigger government can solve any problems.' Fasten your safety belts, says Harris, for '. . . the rudest awakening of all time is at hand': the argument for a market economy '. . . has gained the intellectual ascendancy — on grounds of morality and freedom, even more than efficiency'.

This prophetic article, written four years before Mrs Thatcher's first government achieved office, captures the essence of Ralph's writings and speeches. By 1975, he and Arthur Seldon and the academic authors they mustered had spent almost twenty years working up to a crescendo of criticism of overweening governments whose actions encroached more and more on the freedom of citizens — and in the process led to an economy wasteful in its use of resources. Inflation, unemployment and sterling crises were the symptoms of a deeper malaise afflicting Britain. Their words were beginning to fall on receptive ears and, as yet another crisis loomed, Ralph sensed correctly that Britain was on the verge of radical change.

Although a small collection of articles cannot do justice to the range of Ralph's ideas, it can remind readers of his great talent for entertaining them with radical views, expressed robustly, yet all the time grounded firmly on sound economic principles. Most of his favourite targets figure in this selection which, after 'Cheer up!', reproduces the articles in the order in which they first appeared.

Naturally, politicians and civil servants head the list. From early in the post-war period, he identifies their problem as dependence on the views of defunct economists. They have failed to read and understand Adam Smith, Hayek and (later) Friedman. Consequently, they are bound by the ideas of 1930s Cambridge, over-impressed not just by Keynesian demand-management but believing, following Joan Robinson, that 'imperfections' in markets justify any and every government intervention. Attempts at planning, incomes policies and the other favoured remedies of the 1960s are effectively and vigorously attacked, and the advantages of 'imperfect' competition are demonstrated, in four early articles reprinted here, written between 1965 and 1968 when he and Arthur Seldon were voices in the wilderness. In another early article, from the *Swinton Journal* in 1970, he points out that had Hayek been an 'apostle of collectivism' his seventieth birthday in 1969 would hardly have gone, as it did, virtually unnoticed by the BBC and other organs of opinion.

At the same time that he chastised the politicians, Ralph produced compelling arguments, quite against the conventional wisdom of the day, for the moral superiority of capitalism over socialism. For example, in *The Times* in September 1970 he argued

> '... the first need for our moral health no less than our material well-being is drastically to reduce central power to the minimum that politicians must discharge for security, order and the avoidance of poverty'.

In the early 1970s, Ralph was using short articles in *The Daily Telegraph*, *The Times* and *The Spectator* to explain that high unemployment results not from deficient demand but from the welfare system, from over-powerful trade unions, from minimum-wage provisions and from rent control. And, as the IEA brought to British readers the ideas of Milton Friedman, Ralph spread them to a still wider audience through his newspaper articles. In a *Crossbow* article in 1977, for instance, he asks 'How many billions of pounds of lost output and thousands of unemployed might have been avoided?' if Chancellor Barber had grasped Friedman's point that inflation is always and everywhere a monetary phenomenon and had refrained from inflating the money supply.

As one would expect of a liberal economist, other targets which came under attack were protectionism (a 'costly form of economic warfare that impoverishes all'), the National Economic Development Council (Neddy should be 'carted off to the knacker's yard') and foreign aid (which 'provided incompetent governments with a soft option'). In 1983, impressed by his experience of the legislative process in the House of Lords, in a *Times* article Ralph turns to the need to make government less complex, confining it to '... the barest minimum of functions' and restoring '... politics to a part-time job suitable for gentlemen and lords, that is for unpaid amateurs ...'.

One of Ralph's most prolific periods for short articles was in 1988 when he was writing primarily for *The Sunday Telegraph*. Eight of these articles are reproduced here. They are classic Harris — witty, full of radical ideas and often based on contemporary IEA publications. The bishops are provided with an Easter offering: people should repent of looking to the government for special favours and do competitively as they would be done by. Student loans should be substituted for a large part of the student grant. Education vouchers should be introduced to encourage parent power in schools. Money should be denationalised to avoid political mismanagement.

In these articles, Ralph also returned to deeper philosophical issues. 'Public' services are mostly doomed to failure: self-government in the market-place is inherently superior and caters much better for minorities. 'Do-gooders' are generally destined to do harm, especially in the social welfare field where they increase dependence. Tobacco abolitionists who encourage intolerance are a '. . . more lethal threat to the sum of human welfare than the worst smoking can do to any of us'.

Hayek and 'Austrian School' discovery processes are never far from his mind and are mentioned in many of his papers. In November 1988 he returned specifically to Hayek (in this case, *The Fatal Conceit*), suggesting that his readers ponder 'the miracle of the economic order'. *The Fatal Conceit* was featured in another *Sunday Telegraph* article in February 1991 when he pointed to the dangers of the 'social market' concept then being adopted by 'closet collectivists'.

Mrs Thatcher's achievements were reviewed in *The Independent* in March 1990 — she owed 'a large debt to ideas' but she 'alone took courage to prick the bubble'. In Europe she stood against creeping socialism (*The Sunday Telegraph*, April 1989): others, with less courage, would 'hide behind her skirt and keep quiet, confident in the knowledge that in the last resort she will use the veto . . .'. On the eve of Maastricht in December 1991, with Mrs Thatcher gone, Ralph urged Mr Major not to be '. . . stampeded into signing up for political and monetary union'. He could see no reason to enter on 'political and monetary experiments' which went far beyond freeing trade and factor movements. In June 1993, he pointed again to the dangers of Maastricht and, in particular, to '. . . the obsession with an irreversible monetary union [which] threatens to reduce economic self-government to empty ceremonial'.

Others have explained the influence on ideas which Ralph Harris and Arthur Seldon exerted through their work in the IEA. In this volume, our purpose is to remind Ralph's many admirers of the significant individual contribution which he made to overcoming the collectivist consensus through a series of entertaining, lucid and perspicacious short articles in which he clung tenaciously to classical liberal ideas when nearly all around him believed in various forms of 'planning'. For many years he swam against the tide. But then, remarkably, he helped to make the tide turn. For that, we are all in his debt.

As in all Institute publications, the views expressed in this Occasional Paper are those of the author, not of the IEA (which has no corporate view), its Trustees, Directors or Advisers.

November 1994

COLIN ROBINSON
Editorial Director, Institute of Economic Affairs;
Professor of Economics, University of Surrey

Ralph Harris: A Personal Note

To understand the impact of Ralph's life's work one needs to understand many things about his times, his colleagues, the strategies they adopted and the resources they had at their command. Let me here mention just three matters, one a piece of history, the other two, some little known aspects of his work. They are little known to his fellow countrymen but well recognised overseas.

First, one has to have a sense of the intellectual atmosphere of the post-World War Two era which Ralph Harris and Arthur Seldon, at the bidding of the late Sir Antony Fisher, set out to change. Planning was in; markets were out. The People's War (so called because so many had been involved) had indeed become the People's Peace. As in war, so in peace, the government would run everything. Talk of markets was akin to swearing in church. And when Antony recruited Ralph (who in turn through Lord Grantchester soon found Arthur) the big joke of the day was that Antony had hired 'Britain's last two free-market economists'. They set out to stop a seemingly overwhelming tidal wave, a tsunami even of anti-market thinking, and their success is now well-documented in Richard Cockett's mistitled *Thinking the Unthinkable: Think-Tanks and the Economic Counter-Revolution, 1931-1983* (HarperCollins, 1994). I say 'mistitled' because his history stops not at 1983 but at 1993.

Second, one has to think of their creation, the IEA, not as a narrowly British institute, but rather as an international institution which just happens to be based in London. Its books are sold in over 90 countries every year now and every few days a permission to reprint or translate is issued to an overseas publisher. On a recent visit to the IEA, Gordon Tullock, the world-renowned economist and co-founder (along with 1986 Nobel Laureate James M. Buchanan) of the Public Choice or Virginia School of Economics, commented to me that his IEA Hobart Paperback (No. 9), *The*

Vote Motive (1976), was without doubt the single most successful piece he had ever written in terms of bringing Public Choice insights to an international audience. It is about to go into a second revised and expanded IEA edition after two printings of the first edition, but more importantly it has been translated at least five times including French, Spanish, Italian, Swedish and Korean editions.

Finally, one has to appreciate Ralph's role as a mentor and role model (or 'hero' as I say whenever I have the pleasure of introducing him to audiences) to the growing family of 'IEAs' around the world — there are now about 100 such institutions in nearly 60 countries. Fisher, having made his fortune with Buxted Chickens, had lost nearly everything in Mariculture Ltd., the Cayman Turtle Farm after so-called 'environmentalists' had its products banned in the USA. But about the mid-1970s businessmen and academics around the world, sensing the IEA's growing impact, started turning to Fisher and Harris for advice: how do we copy the IEA?

Fisher, aged 59 by now, embarked on his fifth career. From fighter pilot, to farmer, to chicken king, to turtle saviour, he now became the world-wide institute entrepreneur, finally creating the Atlas Economic Research Foundation to raise start-up funds and act as a focal point for budding Harrises and Seldons. I followed Fisher as President of that Foundation for five years (1987-1991) and continued his practice of involving Ralph as closely as possible in our mission of establishing IEAs all round the world. He was, more often than not, the keynote speaker at our many workshops. More important, he was always available to counsel our fledglings, even at times having them in residence at the IEA for a period to learn the ropes of our business.

As we salute Ralph with this selection from his many columns on the occasion of his achieving threescore and ten, let us not forget

O the enormity of the task he, Arthur and Antony took on;

O the broader international role of the IEA; and

O Ralph's pivotal role in the birth and growth of so many new 'IEAs' the world over.

So, Happy Birthday, Ralph. Those of us around the world who strive to emulate and build on the success of your work are very much in your debt.

November 1994

JOHN BLUNDELL
General Director,
Institute of Economic Affairs

The Author

RALPH HARRIS was born in 1924 and educated at Tottenham Grammar School and Queens' College, Cambridge. He was Lecturer in Political Economy at St. Andrews University, 1949-56, a leader writer on *The Glasgow Herald*, and was General Director of the Institute of Economic Affairs from 1957 to 1987, when he became Chairman from 1987 to 1989 and subsequently (with Arthur Seldon) Founder President and an Honorary Trustee. Apart from his newspaper and other short articles, he has written for the IEA (with Arthur Seldon) *Hire Purchase in a Free Society*, *Advertising in a Free Society*, *Choice in Welfare*, *Pricing or Taxing?* (Hobart Paper No. 71, 1976), *Not from Benevolence* ... (Hobart Paperback No. 10, 1977), *Over-ruled on Welfare* (Hobart Paperback No. 13, 1979), and *Shoppers' Choice* (Occasional Paper No. 68, 1983). His essay, 'In Place of Incomes Policy', was published in *Catch '76 . . .?* (Occasional Paper 'Special' (No. 47), 1976). He contributed the Epilogue, 'Can Confrontation be Avoided?', to *The Coming Confrontation* (Hobart Paperback No. 12, 1978); and his most recent IEA titles are *The End of Government . . .?* (Occasional Paper No. 58, 1980), *No, Minister!* (Occasional Paper No. 71, 1985), and *Beyond the Welfare State* (Occasional Paper No. 77, 1988).

He is a Trustee of the Wincott Foundation and the Atlas Economic Research Foundation (UK), a member of the Political Economy Club, former President of the Mont Pélerin Society, and a former Council Member of the University of Buckingham. He is Chairman of the Advisory Council of the IEA Health and Welfare Unit, Chairman of the Trustees of the CRCE and British Co-Chairman of ICRET, Moscow.

Ralph Harris was created a Life Peer in July 1979 as Lord Harris of High Cross.

Acknowledgements

THE Institute acknowledges with appreciation the help of the following newspapers, journals and other organisations which gave permission to reproduce articles by Lord Harris they had originally published.

The Daily Telegraph
The Glasgow Herald
The Independent
The Sunday Telegraph
The Times

Crossbow
The Spectator
Swinton Journal
Yesterday, Today and Tomorrow

The British Institute of Management
Confederation of British Industry

Each article carries a note of the original source of publication and the date.

1

Cheer up!
Things are getting worse

'What is being bankrupted before our eyes is the post-war all-party mythology that bigger and bigger government can solve any problems.'

Yesterday, Today and Tomorrow, March/April 1975

IT may not look easy to be an optimist in Britain in 1975. You have to work at it, but it's worth the effort.

You have to start by trying to remember Major Clement Attlee. After 1945 he was all set to usher in the New Jerusalem — welfare state, full employment and all that. 'We will never devalue', said Sir Stafford Cripps, shortly before putting the £ down from $4 to $2·80 in 1949.

By 1951 the electorate turned for relief to 13 years of Tory welfare state, full employment ... There were some little local difficulties, especially with 'stop-go'. But super-Macmillan was always ready: first with 'three wise men', then a national incomes commission, and finally NEDO which would surely put everything right — once and for all. Butskellism and the middle-way for ever?

The voters seemed to twig that all was not well and decided in 1964 that the other socialist party should be given another chance — under that clever man Harold Wilson, bathing in the white heat of a technological revolution. But even if his 'first 100 days' did not actually solve any of the problems, it prepared the way for dynamic George Brown and his National Plan. True, that happened to come unstuck, but there was that young Wedgwood Ben with his IRC which was going to fix Leylands, Upper Clyde ... the 100 days grew into 1,000 days — and nights — which just brought us up to the devaluation of

1

1967. 'Fine-tuning' and 'Finger Tip Control of the Economy' were not doing the trick. But that resourceful Mr Wilson was always ready with his freezes, norms, nil-norms, ceilings — just to show our foreign creditors that we could lick inflation.

By 1970 — with prices rising above 5 per cent and unemployment topping 500,000 — the voters thought it was tough Ted Heath's turn. He really knew what he was up to with all that talk about restructuring our economy, society and what-have-you. 'We will have nothing to do with incomes policies', said tough Ted.

So when the going got rough in 1971, that nice Tony Barber hit on the ingenious plan of spending our way at last to the New Jerusalem: 'go-go' would replace 'stop-stop' and GROWTH would solve all our problems — once and for all.

Ignoring those rude 'monetarists' and their alarmist talk of inflation, handouts and subsidies were squirted in all directions. In 1972 'We-will-never-devalue' Barber floated the pound — which promptly started to sink. As for inflation, Tough Ted was ready with — why, bless you, with an incomes policy to solve all problems — once and for all.

In 1973 that smart Peter Walker announced that all was going splendidly — except for raging inflation, the sinking pound, and mounting debts abroad. There must be some mistake ...

Luckily, clever Mr Wilson was still available in 1974 with the final solution. It was so simple. In return for doing everything the TUC wanted, the unions would show us — once and for all — how socialism could really be made to work ...

So by 1975 we can at last sit back and contemplate the wondrous New Jerusalem. Behold! The welfare state is a seething mass of grievances, nationalised industries in turmoil, companies brought to the verge of insolvency, public spending above 55 per cent of GNP, the pound going under for the third time, foreign debts mortgaging our future, unemployment mounting towards one million, inflation roaring above 20 per cent and national bankruptcy staring us in the face.

'Bankruptcy' — of what? Not of the skills, resources, enterprise of the British people. They have survived the assault and battery of government mismanagement. What is being bankrupted before your eyes is the post-war, all-party mythology that bigger and bigger government can solve any problems. If we are ready, 1975 should give those of us who never believed it a chance to prove our case. The Adam Smith, Hayek, Friedman argument for a market economy has gained the intellectual ascendancy — on grounds of morality and freedom, even more than efficiency.

'Oh yes', say the pessimists, 'but the masses will never learn except by experience'. Very well, fasten your safety belts and cheer up: the rudest awakening of all time is at hand.

2

Marketing Pharmaceutical Products

Extracts from a paper presented at a British
Institute of Management Consultation
on Pharmaceutical Marketing
British Institute of Management, 1965

THE younger generation of academic economists developed the idea of 'imperfect competition' from a technical concept to a kind of moral judgement that implied a departure from some ideal. If competition was 'imperfect' ought we not make every effort to identify and remove the blemishes? The hunt was on and a succession of otherwise sensible men began to assail advertising, packaging, branding and above all the wicked differentiation of products. The impracticable absurdity of the exercise would scarcely merit comment were it not that confusions about 'imperfect competition' continue to inflame and distort discussion of economic structure, activity and policy.

The Case for 'Imperfect' Competition
The fundamental error of much modern economic discussion is the assumption that we now know what assortment of goods should be produced — or that we (or the National Economic Development Council) can find the people who do know and get them to tell us once and for all. But by definition a dynamic economy involves change: economic growth has never meant simply turning out larger numbers of *given* products: more bread, more Model T Fords, more bar soap and scrubbing boards, more quill pens, more fly-papers, more poultices, senna pods, or aspirin B.P. The paths of progress in products old and new are various, but an awful lot boils down to something akin to what

in medicine is often criticised as 'molecular manipulation'. What is the latest Rolls-Royce but the old Model T in 'elegant form and vehicle'!

It is because none of us has perfect knowledge about the present (let alone infallible foresight) that we need an open system for pooling intelligence, judgement and hunch to discover the best ways of improving the assortment of products and techniques, all the while testing new ways of catering for the variety of consumer conditions, resistances and preferences. This pooling is best achieved by competition and competitive marketing which is itself a continuing process of empirical research about improved products, techniques, and forms of consumption. It is the imperfections in our knowledge and understanding that argue most strongly for open-ended competition, involving endless experimentation and accompanied by the wastes that are inherent in finding better (but still 'imperfect') ways of achieving our purposes and discarding methods which only by competition can be proved less efficient.

The general lesson I draw from all this is that whilst we should be vigilant to identify and remove avoidable, man-made obstacles to competition, we should, as Hayek has said:*

'worry much less whether competition in a given case is perfect and worry much more whether there is competition at all.'

Marketing — the Hub of Competition

All the economic processes of competition come to a focus in the market-place, just as in political democracy the highly imperfect competition between two or three brands of salvation come to a focus in the ballot booth (once every four or five years, be it noted). However well a firm's techniques of manufacture have developed (in competition with others, needless to say), it must decide what and how much to produce *in anticipation of demand*, not in response to a 'given demand'. All the earlier calculations about research, investment, manufacturing methods, formulation are put to the test, or if you like put to the vote of consumers, in the act of marketing. The outcome must always be to some extent uncertain, since even in basic industries conditions of supply or demand are never static, as Lord Robens and

*'The Meaning of Competition', in *Individualism and Economic Order*, London: Routledge, 1949.

Dr Beeching have painfully discovered. But in modern, emerging industries, where product innovation and obsolescence occur at a rapid and totally unpredictable rate, the uncertainties attending the marketing of new products (or even old products in competition with new) stand out in the sharpest possible contrast to the relatively predictable processes of factory production.

In these circumstances the decisive risk-taking, risk-reducing function which earlier economists entitled the 'entrepreneurial' function, comes to be exercised above all in the sphere of marketing. The economic centre of gravity in industries generally has moved forward from production to marketing as the economy has progressed to cater for the more varied, refined, sophisticated, individual, specific requirements and preferences of consumers with an increasing element of discretionary income. In short, the entrepreneurial function coincides ever more closely with the marketing function, and the marketing function moves from middle to top management.

3
Planning by profits or prophets?

Belief in central planning implies a certain knowledge of the true aims and priorities of economic activity yet this certain knowledge and foresight do not exist. Obviously we must plan. The intelligent question is whether economic planning is best performed by a single central authority or dispersed among many individuals and groups, including public and private authorities, within some general institutional framework that will dovetail together these separate but related plans.'

British Industry, 22 January 1965

IT is easy to make fun of Mr Wilson's '100 days' — now happily coming to an end. Yet the idea of a succession of immediate, far-reaching decisions that would transform the direction of our economic activities follows inevitably from the belief in central planning. Clearly, to accuse 'blind market forces' of producing the wrong things and pursuing false priorities must imply that the critic knows what should be produced and what are the true priorities. Unless he knows, or honestly thinks he knows, the right answers, his criticisms are without visible foundation. And if he does know the right priorities, the sooner central planning is asserted to enforce them the quicker our economic ills will be cured. Indeed, why wait 100 days — or even 10?

The reason, of course, is that, despite years of talk about, for example, import saving, Mr Wilson does not know what we could produce more cheaply at home rather than buy from abroad. Indeed, if he had known all these years, he need not have waited to become Prime Minister to tell us. He could have set an example, advanced the public interest — and made (or should I say 'earned') a whacking profit — by getting into business (whether as economic adviser or entrepreneur) and increasing the production of cheap domestic substitutes for those machine tools or other foreign goods that were mistakenly being imported. If market forces are so blind, those with sight, or second sight, should be able wonderfully to lighten our darkness.

This simple example is doubly revealing. In the first place, it suggests that the assumption of superior knowledge, for example, about comparative costs, on which much of the argument for central planning rests, lacks empirical foundation. In the second place, it emphasises that if better or cheaper sources of home supply can be revealed, central direction would not be necessary to ensure that they were exploited. The publication of information could be expected to awaken users to the existence of cheaper sources of supply and stimulate domestic producers to cater for the resulting increase in home demand. Likewise, if the central planners can show that investment is inadequate to increase productivity, or how far business education would improve managerial efficiency, which new techniques would most reduce costs, or where more computers would more than earn their keep, it would seem that they have only to publicise the relevant data in order to get competitive firms to plan their own businesses on the most enlightened and efficient basis.

But all that this preliminary discussion amounts to is the self-evident proposition that there would be less misdirection of effort and resources if only we possessed fuller information about consumer preferences and the alternative means and costs of supplying them, which involves knowing more about the optimum combination of specific materials, manpower, machinery and marketing methods for producing all types of goods and services.

Perfect Knowledge Unattainable

As soon as we pose this proposition it becomes clear that complete information even of the recent past — let alone of the present or future — is unattainable. Even an expert under the most refined system of the division of labour cannot attain what might be called perfect knowledge — much less perfect foresight. It follows that all plans — private or public — which involve committing resources to specific uses, the outcome of which will be reliably known only afterwards, must involve the risk of error and loss. Thus the installation of a new machine depends on estimates of future demands for the output (volume and price) and of the future course of costs of inputs and of alternative methods of production. When we reflect how variously costs and prices may be influenced by technical, psychological, political, military, trading, population and other changes, we may find cause for wonder that we have survived, let alone enjoyed the most flourishing decade of economic progress this century, with so much reliance on 'blind market forces'.

The explanation is to be found partly in a neglected merit of the broad system of competitive markets which compensates for some of its more apparent shortcomings. Thus a large part of the success of a dynamic economy depends on making the best use of economic data about the alternative employment of scarce resources to produce goods and services efficiently in anticipation of the final demand of hundreds of millions of consumers in Britain and our export markets overseas. The question is not whether to employ planning, since without foresight and design in matching resources to requirements there must be total confusion and chaos. The intelligent question is whether economic planning is best performed by a single central authority or dispersed among many individuals and groups, including public and private authorities, within some general institutional framework that will dovetail together these separate but related plans.

How to Plan

Leaving aside the political dispute about individual freedom versus the concentration of power, the economic merits of these opposed systems would turn on which might be expected to make the fullest use of available knowledge. In the scientific area it may be thought easy to

9

assemble the experts who can command the knowledge relevant for various economic policies, although even here there is the problem of choosing which experts to consult and which to disregard as nonconformists or cranks. But over the larger part of the economy knowledge is widely scattered among individuals with incomplete and often contradictory information about techniques, stocks, supplies, substitutes, market opportunities, special circumstances, local conditions, new facilities and individual skills. The question posed by Professor Hayek almost 20 years ago is:[1]

> 'Not how we can "find" the people who know best, but rather what institutional arrangements are necessary in order that the unknown persons who have knowledge specially suited to a particular task are most likely to be attracted to that task.'

Hayek's answer is worth pondering at a time when Mr George Brown, Mr Frank Cousins, Sir Robert Shone, Professor Stone and others are all bent on precisely the task of trying to 'find the people who know best', which Hayek rejects. His solution to the problem of securing the best use of knowledge is by competitive markets which leave the field open for anyone with a relevant contribution or a clue to missing information. Hayek regards markets as organisations for using and spreading information on which buyers and sellers can act so as between them to make the best use of economic resources. And competition further enables us to review the results and pass continuous judgement on all the participants. The contrasting, currently fashionable, approach is to try to cram all the relevant information necessary for central planning into the heads of a few experts, an exercise which will prove impossible even with the help of computers. Readers in doubt about the impossibility should re-read Mr Owen Hooker's article in the *FBI Review*, October 1964, particularly the significant singling out of 'lack of data' as the major weakness of Professor Stone's SAM (Social Accounting Matrix) model at Cambridge.

The critical importance of information arises mainly from the very fact of economic change. If techniques, population, demand stood still, economic activity would settle into a 'same again' pattern in which

---

[1] 'The Meaning of Competition', reprinted in *Individualism and Economic Order*, London: Routledge & Kegan Paul, 1949.

10

TABLE 1: **Changes in labour force between 1954 and 1962**

	% Increase or Decrease
Total civil employment	+ 6
Engineering, electrical	+23
Paper, printing, publishing	+19
Vehicles	+12
Distribution	+12
Textiles	−18
Coalmining, quarrying	−18
Shipbuilding, marine engineering	−17
Agriculture, forestry, fishing	−13

habit and custom took the place of decision and direction. An unfortunate consequence of the Keynesian revolution has been that economists have increasingly tended to play down or ignore continuous small changes which even in the not-very-long-run can add up to decisive redirection in methods and output. The fashionable concentration on macro-economics at the expense of rigorous micro-analysis has led to a growing pre-occupation with statistical aggregates which display a deceptive stability and mask significant changes in their constituent parts. How else could the British economy in the past decade have come to be plausibly written off as 'stagnant' if we had noticed the remarkable advances in chemicals, fibres, building, electronics, cars and other consumer durables, and no doubt in many smaller categories, which were buried beneath the average 2½ per cent annual increase in GNP? Table 1 summarises some of the remarkable changes in the broad groups of employment over as short a term as eight years.

Planning for Change

Who could have foreseen these changes? And who knows what effect changing techniques, productivity, markets will have on the labour force by 1970? Incidentally, if you dwell on these questions too long, you may begin to wonder how an incomes policy can be devised which would not frustrate those very changes in relative wages and profits which have helped to bring about this re-allocation of labour and other resources to exploit changing techniques, costs, demands and prices.

The dilemma about forecasts like Neddy's 4 per cent growth rate is not merely that most are quickly exploded, but that we can never be sure that they may not be proved unexpectedly right for the wrong reasons. There have certainly been some spectacular misforecasts like the groundnuts scheme, the adverse terms of trade argument, the fuel gap, the decline in population, the steel programme, early atomic energy calculations, the perpetual dollar shortage, all of which provided the basis for mistaken Government economic policies.[2] My favourite example of the difficulties that beset forecasters is drawn from the Ridley Committee on fuel and power resources. In 1951, acting on what it considered the most reliable technical and economic advice, it offered its 'best estimate of the pattern and scale of consumption' 10 years on.

The Committee was quite near the mark on the total fuel consumption by 1961. Its estimates for the individual industries, however, were wildly out: which did not help producers, who are not interested in the demand expressed as 'coal equivalent tons' but in the market for their particular fuel.

The relevance of all this for the choice between planning from the centre and planning through competitive markets suggests lessons for both Labour and Conservative economists. Both should see the advantage of policies that will improve the supply of information for public and private decision-takers. Thus, official statistics should be improved, speeded-up and published with fuller and franker acknowledgement of margins of error, omissions, and of qualitative variations which defy accurate measurement. At the same time, legal requirements for disclosure by public and private companies should be widened to include information on classified turnover, stocks, capital valuations, marketing expenditure and other business operations discussed by Mr Harold Rose in his celebrated Eaton Paper.[3]

In the light of Hayek's view of markets as a source of information,

---

[2] A sobering account of some recent forecasting efforts will be found in C. Pratten, 'The Best-Laid Plans . . .', *Lloyds Bank Review*, July 1964.

[3] *Disclosure in Company Accounts*, London: Institute of Economic Affairs. revised edition, February 1965.

public policy should accept freer movements in relative prices (and profits) as an essential feature of a dynamic economy in which variations in costs direct resources from low-yield uses into openings where their contribution to consumer satisfaction will be higher. It is movements in prices which inform and help to co-ordinate the dispersed planning decisions of firms, public bodies and individuals. If the supply of tin is reduced, or demand for it increased (e.g. by substitution of tin for glass or cardboard), users do not need to be lectured about the reasons, nor exhorted to economise tin. Its price will rise to whatever extent is necessary to keep enough marginal buyers out of the market, and/or to release stocks to meet the swollen demand. Unfortunately, inflation often masks such changes in relative prices which should serve as altimeters or speedometers to help regulate the decisions of the scattered army of entrepreneurs, managers, traders, consumers whose individual plans must be brought into relationship within the total market of available resources.

I am not here concerned with the Government's rôle to balance out the economy by avoiding excessive demand or excessive unused capacity, beyond emphasising three shortcomings of Conservative monetary and fiscal management which look like being perpetuated under the new Government. First, public expenditure ought to be variable downwards in order to offset unforeseen increases in demands on resources arising from investment, foreign trade and even consumer spending which otherwise set up one-way pressures for inflation, balance-of-payments trouble and devaluation. Secondly, as Mr Christopher Dow has shown,[4] Government policy has more often than not upset the economy by errors of short-term forecasting which have led to the exaggeration first of the upswings and then of the checks on total demand. What a dynamic economy requires is an easier hand on the reins and more margins of safety in foreign reserves, capacity, employment, mobility, Government expenditure, to absorb short-term variations in demand for final output.

Burden of Change

Thirdly, by courting inflation that destroys all safety margins, the Government have constantly thrown the burden of adjustment on to

[4] *Management of the British Economy 1945-1960*, Cambridge University Press, 1964.

the hard-pressed private sector (60 per cent only of the economy) by taxing companies, imposing purchase tax on selected products, varying hire purchase terms, first giving and then snatching back tax concessions on new investment, and alternating a cheap money policy with sudden lurches to 7 per cent. All these stop-gap policies are examples of Government-imposed disturbances on business information which make private *planning for profit* more difficult and expose public *planning by prophets* to the sort of disenchantment that Neddy has suddenly encountered from Mr Michael Shanks and other former disciples.

If a Labour Government think they know better than businessmen in one industry or another, it is preferable for them to take over a firm or establish a public enterprise as pace-setter in free competition for profit with other firms, rather than exhort, bribe or compel the whole industry to act on the central planner's information, which we have shown must be incomplete.

If the Conservatives want an intelligent alternative to the pretensions of central planning, they should reconsider the requirements of a competitive market economy, drawing on a distinguished line of scholars including Marshall and Keynes, and among whom Professors Lord Robbins, F. A. Hayek, John Jewkes, B. S. Yamey, Colin Clark, Frank Paish, G. C. Allen and A. R. Prest are fortunately still very much alive.

If businessmen come to decide that, after all, they like central planning less than risk-taking private enterprise, they will have to stop looking for Government favours and look more to self-help. They can do this by avoiding rigid restrictive practices, welcoming fuller disclosure of business information, and tackling the risks of an uncertain future with the help of better market research and more flexible advertising and pricing policies. There is also scope for a variety of insurance hedging contracts, and other neglected devices that would reduce risks or transfer them to specialists in speculation. Such a reconstruction of competitive markets could bring better planning by reference to making profits (or minimising losses) than by reference to false prophets with their flawed crystal balls.

4

When the Price is Right

Devaluation has forced the Government to admit the central importance of market pricing, even for a country's currency. Here is the case for pricing throughout the economy.

The Daily Telegraph, 21 November 1967

SUPPOSE Mr Aubrey Jones, now awakening to the futility of periodic edicts on the price of bread, milk, detergents, haircuts and newspapers, stalked into the nearest supermarket and shuffled the price tags round in accord with his vision of 'the public interest'. It takes no economic genius to predict confusion, with queues to buy up the bargains and piles of over-priced goods left unsold.

Such a far-fetched experiment would at least have the merit of exposing in a single stride the distortion and ultimate disruption of economic activity towards which we are at present merely shuffling. If today the fortunes of coal, electricity, railways and even newspapers are heading for crises that politicians euphemistically call 'major adjustments', it is because for years their prices and costs have not been permitted to reflect changes in conditions of supply and demand.

Imagine how much bleaker the post-war years would have been if the 'planners' had stopped the prices of plastics, artificial fibres, antibiotics, chicken, ballpoints and detergents, washing machines and television sets from falling in relation to the prices of their old-fashioned substitutes.

Indispensable Guide

Short-sighted politicians might be excused for embracing the will-of-the-wisp of prices and incomes policy as a smokescreen for their failure to stop sowing the seeds of inflation, to weed-out restrictive practices, and to prune the sprawling public sector. More puzzling is the cavalier attitude of many professional economists towards the system of market pricing which Professor James Meade, writing as a 'liberal-socialist', once described as 'among the greatest social inventions of mankind'.

The paradox is that pricing is the pivot of economic analysis and action. It is to the economist what the slide-rule and scales are to the scientist or, more dynamically, what the instrument panel is to the test pilot. Who can say whether scarce resources are efficiently applied unless he can measure and compare their yields in alternative uses? Even in a not very competitive economy like Britain's, the catalogue of relative prices represented by rates of interest, profits, wages, provides an indispensable guide to getting existing savings, risk capital, labour, from less efficient to more efficient employments.

Our stubborn economic problems stem from the failure to understand and apply the logic of pricing as the regulator of supply and demand. Regional unemployment could be tackled by moving away from national wage rates so as to cheapen labour in depressed areas, as the Government's payroll subsidy has belatedly and indirectly acknowledged.

It is even possible that the worst of the brain drain could be avoided by raising the price for brains at this end. Most of the reasons given for emigration in the Jones Report — better prospects, facilities, conditions — are simply euphemisms for more money. But even if non-monetary attractions like sunshine and elbow-room accounted for the flow of British talent to the United States, it would not mean that financial recompense was ruled out. Indeed, the less we can do about the British weather, the more we should rely on the relative counter-attractions of higher income and lower taxes, about which we can do much.

Perhaps the most convincing demonstration of the pivotal importance of pricing is the mess we get into when prices are artificially reduced or eliminated altogether — as in the social services. Contrast the ample provision of what Mr Wilson used to deride as 'candy floss' with the inadequate supply of what all politicians like to describe as 'free' welfare.

We are not short of entertainments, or hi-fi, or garden furniture, or fashion wear, or (till the Government clamped down) of foreign holidays, or of any goods and services which are permitted to be bought and sold commercially at prices that cover their costs. In sharpest contrast, we are short of most 'public' goods and services. We always seem to need more doctors, teachers, hospitals, schools, subsidised council houses. What is missed by the economic Bourbons but as plain as a pikestaff to the market economist is that whenever valued goods or services are offered at zero price, demand will be inflated and supply attenuated.

Nor can the egalitarian console himself that if 'free' services lead to lower standards, at least all suffer equally. In practice, the most vicious kind of free-for-all flourishes beneath the surface of 'fair shares' in the Welfare State. Doing away with pricing does not dispose of scarcity: limited supplies still have to be rationed among competing customers by some device or other.

The Pick of the Draw

In state schooling, even under so-called 'comprehensive' equality, it is the parent who can afford to move to the right 'catchment area' whose children will get the pick of a very mixed bag. With subsidised council houses it is the luck of the draw, depending on local administrative rules and the possibility of getting round them. With expensive life-saving equipment like the artificial kidney machine, the chance of a patient's survival may turn — as does much else — on the push or prominence of his relatives.

'Rationing by the purse' may sound a hard-headed doctrine, although it can be softened by putting more cash (or vouchers) in the lightest purses. But who would knowingly vote for what might be called 'rationing by the pat on the back' whereby those with the best contacts, the right accent, the tallest story, the biggest bribe (or smallest conscience), may get the lion's share of whatever 'free' goods and services are going? The fallacy of abandoning pricing is that the neediest may benefit least while the better-off or politically well-connected wrangle their way to the top. A lottery is always more capricious than an auction.

It was the widespread neglect of such economic analysis that prompted the Institute of Economic Affairs last year to launch an essay competition for young economists on 'the scope of pricing in maximising the efficiency of resources'. The essays of the winners and runners-up were published yesterday in a volume* that focuses attention on pricing as a weapon in our struggle against waste, inefficiency, rigidity, lethargy and other symptoms of the 'English disease'.

The significance of this collection of 14 essays is to show that pricing can help solve an infinite variety of problems, minor or major, ranging from refuse disposal, fire-protection, water supply, seaside amenities, and egg marketing, to the broad issues of central planning, taxation and agricultural policy.

Economic Realism

The essay by a Bradford University lecturer shows how the average cost of electricity might be reduced by charging higher rates at peak periods. Here is a nationalised industry with £4,000 million of precious capital, investing more than £700 million a year and earning a paltry net return of 5 per cent, compared with 14 per cent in private industry. By charging the same rate on a cold winter night as on midsummer eve (when costs are much lower) the industry has to install new capacity and keep high-cost old plant running in a desperate effort to avoid power cuts in periods of exceptional demand. The author's solution of seasonal variations in price would leave the consumer to decide whether to pay the high costs of supply at peak periods or to economise demand and enable the industry to reduce its costs.

It is precisely the neglect of such economic realism that has paved the way to devaluation and needs more urgently than ever to be put right.

The reader of this volume may think of other applications of pricing — in pay-television, public libraries, art galleries, opera, the post office, Civil Service salaries, and throughout the social services. What such fearless economic analysis demonstrates is that the neglect of pricing, particularly throughout the public sector, causes or aggravates more problems than politicians can ever hope to solve without its help. When Government is piling compulsion on cajolery

*Essays in the Theory and Practice of Pricing, Institute of Economic Affairs, 1967, 25s.

18

in a vain effort to suppress the price system, it may seem perverse to emphasise its incomparable efficiency. Yet, as disillusioned economists in Eastern Europe have learned the hard way, so long as 'planning' tries to prevail against 'supply and demand' — that is, the wishes of people as suppliers and demanders — no battery of computers or coercion will prevent consequent confusion and even chaos.

5

Grave-diggers of planning

The Glasgow Herald, 8 February 1968

DISILLUSIONMENT with Mr Wilson and all his works should cause no more than modified rapture for those who care most deeply about the health of a free society.

Massive as his guilt may be, we are inviting trouble in the future if we overlook the responsibility of so many others for the phoney policies which date back to 1961, although they have only now finally collapsed on our heads. The alarming lesson is that most politicians of all parties, the majority of business 'leaders' at the CBI, and the more articulate journalists, broadcasters, academic publicists, and opinion-formers only began to question the planning swindle after the entire house of cards fell about their credulous ears.

'We Told You So'

Indeed, among politicians, who but Enoch Powell and his friends are entitled to say, 'We told you so?'. In November 1965, eight months before the hasty interment of George Brown's and Mr Callaghan's 'vision for the future', the Conservative (and Liberal) 'leaders' in the Commons accepted without a division the resolution: 'That this House welcomes the National Plan'.

In his new book* Professor Jewkes has no difficulty in demonstrating the total failure of the NEDC plan which Macmillan launched with the confident aim of conjuring up a steady 4 per cent annual growth in output from 1961-66. Instead, in the five years growth ranged from under 1 per cent to over 5 per cent and averaged less than 3 per cent as in the bad old days of 'stop-go'. The errors in

*John Jewkes, *The New Ordeal by Planning*, is published today (London: Macmillan, 1968, 42s).

specific targets, like investment, exports, earnings, were even more laughably and perversely wide of the mark.

Before Conservative apologists wriggle with talk that Neddy at least did no harm, Professor Jewkes points out that it was misplaced belief in the 'plan' which darkened counsel and delayed remedial measures in the inflationary boom of 1964. Likewise, under the new Labour Government, obsession with the even more ambitious National Plan distracted attention away from the sombre realities of impending disaster and put policy (particularly on Government expenditure) into a straitjacket from which even Mr Jenkins showed himself last month still unable to escape.

If this book was simply a post-mortem with the aid of hindsight, the first 40 pages would provide a valuable summary of what went wrong in the 1960s. But it is very much more. For good measure the remaining 200 pages reproduce the greater part of a brilliant book, *Ordeal by Planning*, which he first published in 1948 after top-level experience of planning in war.

Twenty years after first reading this exposé of the inevitable failure of such 'short-cuts' as central economic planning I am more than ever impressed by the quality of the author's analysis, his sure grasp of essentials, his wise acknowledgement of fallible human understanding, and his flowing clarity of exposition. Thus on the noble aspirations of (some) planners for a more humane, secure, scientific, just society, Jewkes pointed out that such legitimate hopes are in practice self-frustrating:

'For central planning ultimately turns every individual into a cipher and every economic decision into blind fumbling, destroys the incentives through which economic progress arises, renders the economic system as unstable as the whims of the few who ultimately control it, and creates a system of wire-pulling and privileges in which economic justice ceases to have any meaning.'

If planning has failed everywhere — and is being reversed even in Communist economies — why are so many 'sophisticated' people taken in? Professor Jewkes diagnosed — in 1948 — several sources of confusion in human weakness: 'The turbulent craving for a new order of things' (how's that for George Brown or Dr Balogh?); 'an itch for novelty' (the occupational hazard of journalists); 'a remarkably oversimplified conception of the task which lies before them' (Callaghan and Wilson); 'exaggeration of the benefits to be derived from mechanisation' (Wedgwood Benn, Wilson, and other 'technological' addicts); 'a strong predilection for tidiness in the economic system' (Aubrey Jones, Fred Catherwood, and the restless tribe of tinkerers).

'Superficial Appeal of Planning'

The superficial appeal of planning owes much to the greater intellectual effort required to grasp the more subtle, complex, wide, and long-range considerations in favour of a free economy, which the author illustrates vividly from his own capacious knowledge of the indispensable role of the entrepreneur and the practical working of the price system. Many who might resist the Utopian claims of planning fall victim to the more plausible argument that more of it is necessary in a mixed economy. Hence the 'economic appeasers' who pride themselves on having a 'balanced and judicial mind'.

> 'Yet no democratic community can exist save where its members understand the difference between having their hair cut short and having their scalps taken clean off, and recognise in the former the ever-growing dangers of the latter.'

The central reason for rejecting economic planning is not because the planners are incompetent but because what they are attempting is impossible. To stand any chance of success a central economic plan would call for a degree of understanding we do not have about the precise ingredients of growth, complete knowledge of all available resources, absolute power to control and relate myriad components accordingly, supernatural powers to predict changes in techniques and consumer preference.

Politicians Decide

Even if the theory of central planning were less ramshackle, Jewkes reminds us that it is *politicians* who decide the plans in the light of ill-considered election commitments, and it is 'comically naïve' to expect Wilson, Jenkins, or even Heath to allow the economic or statistical experts to try to determine the planning of output or employment *objectively* — without calculating (however wrongly) the response of trade unions, farmers, MPs, marginal voters, the regions, and other lobbies. Hence the descent from the high theory of planning to the low-down.

No review can do justice to a book which packs into 240 pages more wisdom and constructive thought than could be gleaned from the mostly barren literature of planning during the 20 years the author bestrides with such easy mastery. And let the non-economist also buy or borrow from the nearest library a book which attacks the obsessive materialism of those who would have us devote all our waking lives to a vain effort to rescue their plan from its inevitable doom. The truth is that the planners are digging their own grave and this book shows how we can hasten the funeral and resume the neglected task of reconstructing the free economy on surer foundations.

6

On Hayek

Extracts from *Swinton Journal*, Spring 1970

HAD Hayek been an apostle of collectivism instead of its most lethal living opponent, his 70th birthday would have been the signal for the whole apparatus of press, radio and television to rejoice in the presence among us of a truly great thinker. The BBC would have vied with the *New Statesman* to mark 1969 not only as the 70th anniversary of Hayek's birth (in Vienna) but symbolically as the 25th of the publication of *The Road to Serfdom*. On the latter event, one can picture Robin Day, David Dimbleby and all the other up-to-the-minute men interviewing victims of collectivist oppression in Russia, China, Czechoslovakia, Cuba and some of the newer African countries to test Hayek's thesis that political control over the means of production, distribution and exchange inevitably extinguishes individual freedom in political no less than in economic affairs.

Contrast the audible silence which greeted Hayek's double anniversary with the tributes showered in their lifetime on such now largely forgotten socialist folk heroes as G. D. H. Cole, Hugh Dalton, Harold Laski and even R. H. Tawney. More specifically, contrast the slender basis of intellectually reputable writing that has made J. K. Galbraith into the undergraduate equivalent of a matineé idol and brought him an invitation to Trinity in the university of Marshall, Keynes, Pigou and Robertson. The survival of belief in the free economy against such one-sided attention testifies to the power of ideas and to the practical failure of the opposing philosophy to supply a tolerable alternative.

Hayek's most exacting admirers may doubt whether *The Road to Serfdom* is his best claim to fame, but a re-reading will satisfy most sceptics that it combines more intellectual force, analytical subtlety and mature wisdom than all Galbraith's superficially more appealing works put together. Indeed, from a list of well over 100 essays in Hayek's repertoire, single efforts like 'The Meaning of Competition' or 'The Use of Knowledge in Society' throw more light on the indispensable rôle of the market mechanism than a bookshelf of more widely known and acclaimed volumes in the libraries of many university departments of social science.

If we can still rely on profound ideas having a larger (though later) impact on events than more shallow, showy 'new thinking', there need be no undue anxiety that the contemporary world appears largely to be ignoring Hayek's contribution to politics, economics and philosophy. But if his genius must await posthumous recognition by the many, it is a modest consolation that some of the few who have grasped his importance should meanwhile honour his 70th birthday by a volume of essays entitled *Roads to Freedom.** None of Hayek's friends will be wholly satisfied that this *Festschrift* does full justice to the man it celebrates, despite characteristic contributions by Popper, Lutz, Paish, Buchanan, Haberler, Machlup, Bauer and half-a-dozen other champions of the free market economy. But none, even of his critics, can fail to be impressed by the evidence these 15 essays give of the many-sidedness of Hayek's contribution to theory on the trade cycle, money, interest rates, wages, pricing, planning and competition as well as to the practice of law, political institutions, the scientific method, history and even language in political thought.

---

*Edited by Erich Streissler, Routledge & Kegan Paul, 1969, price £4.

25

7

Let us give two cheers for capitalism

'... even the remnant of capitalism in Britain — though it accounts for whatever success our economy still enjoys — is not safe from further erosion until we can instruct both its practitioners and its critics that competitive enterprise is superior ...'

The Sunday Telegraph, 13 September 1970

IF the issue turned on a purely materialist reckoning, the triumph of capitalism over socialism could hardly be in doubt. Even it we had forgotten the miracle of material progress achieved in the West by largely unguided private enterprise in the 19th century and earlier, the lesson has been hammered home in the post-war years by the contrast between the bustling creation of wealth in Germany, North America or Hongkong, and the drift of persistent poverty throughout India and most of Africa from Egypt to Northern Rhodesia despite the massive transfusion of 'aid'.

In Eastern Europe the poor performance of central planning has forced even Russian Communists to try to bring back the alien concepts of market pricing, enterprise and profitability.

The superiority of capitalism in making the best use of scarce resources is in principle not hard to understand. History is full of examples of countries richly endowed with natural resources, fertile land and favourable climate that have languished until the most vital resource of all, individual enterprise, is unleashed to co-operate in harvesting the latent wealth.

26

Circumstances of course, must be right. The most adventurous innovator will not invest effort and capital in projects yielding their return over many years, unless there is a framework of law and order which promises some security against force and fraud — whether from common thieves, less scrupulous competitors, corrupt officials or grasping governments.

Merits of Competition

Within such a setting, competition must be most effective because it allows better ideas to supersede prevailing ideas by giving them a chance to prove themselves — without seeking the approval of central planners who can never have a monopoly of wisdom to match their monopoly of power. It provides a trial-and-error system open to people with varying talents, knowledge, visions, techniques, effort and perseverance, all seeking ways of making scarce resources go furthest in meeting the demands on them.

Throughout the economy, in welfare, nationalised industries, taxation, land development, atomic energy, transport and broadcasting, public policy is diverted from its most efficient, creative course because of objections on allegedly moral grounds to competitive enterprise and market pricing. In each case, confusion between the motive and the outcome of human action leads to a mis-judgement of market-based policies.

Central to this widespread moral obfuscation is dislike of the appeal to self-interest which it is supposed private enterprise peculiarly exploits. After 25 years' study of the writing of the classical liberal economists from Adam Smith to Keynes, Hayek, Robbins and Milton Friedman, I believe this supposition is without theoretical or empirical foundation.

Particularly during the past decade since resuming regular church-going, I have questioned whether a belief in capitalism conflicts with the best in the Christian ethic. Why do I unhesitatingly prefer the capitalism expounded by Mr Enoch Powell and Sir Keith Joseph to the mixed (or mixed-up) economy of many Conservatives or the socialism of Mr Wilson and Bishop Trevor Huddleston?

At the outset it must be emphasised that so-called self-interest is not simply a result of original sin, but also of fallible knowledge and

27

understanding which limits our comprehension to what best suits our family, friends, neighbourhood, and other specific causes we make our own. Insofar as fallen man generally prefers his own interest in this sense to that of others, the capitalist system, even as practised in the USA, has two decisive advantages over a socialist régime as practised in Russia.

In the first place, as Adam Smith emphasised nearly 200 years ago, competitive markets can harmonise private and social interest by harnessing to productive, creative tasks what he described as 'the uniform, constant and uninterrupted effort of every man to better his condition'. By leading individuals to apply their talents and property where they yield the highest wage, salary, rent, profit, the market system provides a systematic mechanism for getting immensely varied human material resources into employments where they contribute most to what Smith called 'opulence' or 'the wealth of nations'.

No Compulsion

Notice, by the way, that nobody is compelled to maximise his monetary return. Those who prefer leisure, contemplation, voluntary work, getting into the honours list, or other satisfactions can, under capitalism, turn aside from the 'rat race' and maximise whatever combination and forms of income and idleness suits their tastes. Furthermore, although most people will work harder for their families than for whatever passes in peacetime as 'the national interest', they can often best help their favourite good causes by maximising their monetary income so as to afford larger contributions to charities.

It may be more emotionally satisfying for a student to talk of going to Africa during the vacation to involve himself in 'community service' among the natives. But he will probably be highly incompetent at nursing the sick or instructing Africans in better crop and animal husbandry; whereas by staying at home he could easily earn £20 a week as a building labourer and send money to Africa which would do far more good. Into the bargain, he would save his fare which would alone be enough to keep an African family in luxury for a year or more.

Confronted with such realistic alternatives which the market system makes available, the preference of students — and other idealists — for so-called 'community service' is not more moral but merely a disguised form of self-interest or self-indulgence, and one which does less, if any, good to the intended beneficiaries.

The second enormous advantage of capitalism over socialism in dealing with the widespread phenomenon of self-interest is best grasped by dwelling on the following quotation from Keynes:

'... dangerous human proclivities can be canalised into comparatively harmless channels by the existence of opportunities for money-making and private wealth, which, if they cannot be satisfied in this way, may find their outlet in cruelty, the reckless pursuit of personal power and authority.

'It is better that a man should tyrannise over his bank balance than over his fellow citizens; ... The task of transmuting human nature must not be confused with the task of managing it.'

If self-interest — or what I prefer to call 'individual purpose' — is as strong, widespread and persistent as Adam Smith and Keynes believed and as idealistic socialists deplore, how can it be subdued?

Socialist Self-Interest

So far from scorning an appeal to self-interest, from 1964 to 1970 socialist policies have exploited the honours system and extended patronage in the form of subsidies and well-paid prestigious public appointments to divert (or pervert) individual purposes wherever they have been inconvenient to public policy.

Royal Commissions and independent committees have been packed with partisan allies; permissions for firms to merge have been granted in return for undertakings to bolster the political purposes of Ministers; grants from public funds have been used to advance Labour's electoral prospects or to placate trade unions in industries like shipbuilding where restrictive practices have enriched sectional interests and brought firms to the verge of bankruptcy; and following the Budget in 1970 a wages scramble was connived at in order to win short-sighted votes in the June election.

Ministers who denounce private provision as introducing double standards into education or medical care themselves betray a far more culpable dual standard in public profession and personal conduct by patronising private schools and health insurance. Some of the most indignant critics of inequality look to spread a nation of council tenants whilst themselves living in fine style between two or three residences.

The Minister who singled out private employment agencies for attack as a threat to official labour exchanges was simultaneously negotiating with one of them for a house-keeper. And Mr Crossman, who addresses trade union audiences privately as 'brothers', was publicly revealed by the *Daily Telegraph* (5-10 March 1970) as the Minister who kept a first-class railway compartment to himself whilst others were standing in the corridor.

The more power is concentrated at the centre, the more its control becomes the focus of inflated individual self-interest by the ambitious and abject subservience by their victims. Thus, so far from a Socialist party appealing for votes to the most generous and unselfish instincts of the electorate, Mr Wilson (on whose platform Bishops Huddleston and Stockwood have been proud to stand) broke all records in 1964 and 1966 in a blatant appeal to almost universal self-enrichment through increased social benefits without increased taxation. In 1970, we saw the performance further degraded by evasions about past pledges and the monumental example of a Cabinet of mostly honourable men defending their own prospects of power by gerrymandering the constituency boundaries.

The compelling merit of competitive capitalism is that power is widely dispersed so that even the most mighty men in the market-place are subject to continuous review and challenge from competition — or from Government in its absence.

The last word on the moral danger of fattening-up politicians with too much power comes from E. M. Forster in *Two Cheers for Democracy*:

> 'As soon as people have power they go crooked and sometimes dotty as well, because the possession of power lifts them into regions where normal honesty never pays. . . . the more highly public life is organised, the lower does its morality sink.'

Today, the first need for our moral health no less than our material well-being is drastically to reduce central power to the minimum that politicians must discharge for security, order and the avoidance of poverty. In so doing, we will be restoring the individual opportunity, private choice, and personal responsibility that are the indispensable ingredients of a moral order.

8

Stop inflation at its source

The Glasgow Herald, 9 October 1972

To dispel some of the gloom, the saga of inflation might be presented as a variant of the music hall stories on the theme of good news and bad news.

If we are to put the worst news first, it must be that inflation could prove lethal to the free society.

A 10 per cent rise in prices each year is enough to slice the value of the £1 to less than one new penny within a working life of 50 years. A small loaf would then cost about £10.

But long before that stage, settled habits of thrift and prudence would give way to a spending spree that would speed the circulation of money to produce a galloping inflation in which the poor and innocent always lose out to the strong and ruthless.

Then the calm search for remedies would be swamped by calls for vengeance. The recent chorus against 'property speculators' was a tiny foretaste of an evil poison that could dissolve the fabric of ordered society.

Against this spectre must be set better news that an opinion survey commissioned by the Institute of Economic Affairs showed the British public is awakening to the threat of inflation as far more worrying than the old bogey of unemployment.

*   *   *

For good measure, opinion is coming to think trade unions have a large hand in the process and are getting too big for their jackboots.

If Mr Heath wants to salvage one nation, it is not a cosy consensus on policy he should be seeking but a growing unity on the aim to stop inflation at its source.

A more widely held view would be that while a continuing large increase in the circulation of money would suffice to sustain inflation without help from excessive wage awards, the monopoly power of unions backed by damaging strikes simply makes the path of monetary rectitude more daunting for unheroic politicians.

Happily, disagreement on whether to slow the pace of inflation by checking the accelerator (cutting back on money) or by applying the brake (curbing union power) can be resolved by doing both.

We now come to what I regard as the much worse news that the Government is dabbling again with the tempting but vain therapy of incomes policy.

Despite the ingenuity of the latest appeal for a limit of £2 all round, the history of this secular form of the laying on of hands proves it is no alternative to unpalatable medicine and surgery.

Recent experience in many countries confirms that such voluntary endeavours have no large or lasting effect in moderating wage increases.

*   *   *

Indeed, in Britain a succession of plateaus, guidelines, standstills, norms, freezes, and ceilings have paved the way to the present unholy alliance of record inflation and rising unemployment.

These Whitehall parlour games are not only poor economics but bad politics. If, by some gamble against all the odds, this latest sample of Government by Chequers tea-party came off, it would prolong the distortion of relative wages and prices which already diverts too much of our resources into wasteful misemployments.

Above all, it would be a further retreat from the rule of law to the regulation of our affairs by medieval guilds and private cabals which impose their whims by devious pressures on free men guilty of no worse sin than conducting business in the light of their best judgement and according to the law of the land.

So long as they pay lip-service to norms, however, they should be ready this time to deal firmly with the inevitable abnorms which militant trade unionists (or political wreckers) will throw back at them.

Here, Conservatives could not do better than take their cue from a self-confessed liberal-socialist, Professor James Meade, who in his

Wincott lecture last year proposed that unions striking for unacceptable demands should lose their accumulated rights for redundancy pay and have their supplementary benefits either financed by the union or in the form of a loan they would have to repay.

After that bright interval the bad news comes thick and fast. No incomes policy or curb on labour monopolies will touch inflation unless buttressed by a tight rein on the money supply.

It follows remorselessly that public expenditure must be cut back to reduce the budget deficit now financed more or less directly by the printing press.

There is no escape in trying to balance the books by raising taxation, which is already a major independent spur to inflation.

The mischief is revealed with the help of a few figures. A family with two children having no more than 20 debased pounds coming in each week now pays about £2 in taxes.

*　　　*　　　*

On Mr Heath's handout of £2, the breadwinner's tax rate is 35 per cent, so that take-home pay goes up much less than the apparent 10 per cent.

Indeed, for such a family to hold its own in face of a 10 per cent price rise, an increase in gross income of 14 per cent would be needed.

High taxes are thus an inbuilt inflator which can be pricked only by drastic cuts in public spending.

In gloomier moments I confess to seeing Britain becoming a kind of nature reserve for Europe in which are harmlessly preserved every variety of sacred cow, dying duck, nationalised dinosaur, trade union cart horse, and specially fattened underdogs, all jostling at the public feeding trough.

But before this animal farm attracts the rude attention of an Orwellian pig, I fancy we will bestir ourselves and strive for the higher standards of living most of us plainly think worth earning — and even striking for.

Straining for good news, therefore, I interpret the evidence of so much wrong with the British economy as showing scope for just a little less nonsense in one or two directions to yield a galvanising effect.

It is remarkably encouraging news that we have survived thus far, despite the laceration of self-inflicted wounds.

*   *   *

If any forgivably sensitive souls fear we must fail to head off inflation because of the risk of higher unemployment, I conclude with more good news.

While the experts of the Department of Employment were busy cooking up press releases for trusting journalists to make headlines about 1,000,000 on the dole, an Institute of Economic Affairs report took the official statistics apart and found at least half this crude, alarmist total were either unemployable or busy moving between jobs, often cushioned by an untaxed benefit (plus tax repayment) higher than their previous (taxed) take-home pay.

No doubt any solution to inflation will add to the unemployment statistics, particularly if unions try to defy monetary discipline and follow the dockers, miners, printers, and Clydesiders in pricing more of their unfortunate members out of jobs.

But this increase would be the more short-lived if we copy the Swedish example of confining generous unemployment pay to people who retrain for new work. After inflation is mastered, we are left with the task of getting people now in protected, artificial employments to shift to new and expanding firms earning high profits.

9

Who are
the guilty men?

The Spectator, 23 February 1974

SUPPOSE we take a break from the party political shadow-boxing that passes for a mature democracy in action and ask who, if anyone, is responsible for the latest economic assault perpetrated on the poor old pound — with at least 15 per cent inflation generally expected this year.

There would be a number of charges on the sheet but all are subordinate to what might be summarised as economic arson — the setting light to the powder trail of inflation. A full-scale court of inquiry would take time. Meanwhile, at the preliminary hearings any competent judge would dismiss from the case several popular suspects such as property speculators and foreigners, and put the trade union bosses on bail as accessories before or after the fact. On circumstantial evidence, the most likely-looking incendiaries to be hauled up for questioning would certainly be Mr Heath, his Chancellor Anthony Barber, and that unquenchable prophet of boom, Peter Walker.

There are now very few expert witnesses who would seriously challenge the empirical evidence Milton Friedman has assembled from many countries over long periods of history, irrespective of trade union power or government controls, that

'inflation is always and everywhere a monetary phenomenon in the sense that it is and can be produced only by a more rapid increase in the quantity of money than in output.'

After consulting his customary advisers Mr Heath might plead that in the past when money supply was momentarily cut back, prices went on rising; but his objection would be over-ruled by reference to any standard monetary text which emphasises under some such heading as 'lagged response' that the first impact of a change in the quantity of money is on the level of real output for up to nine months with the major effect on the rate of inflation taking nearer 18 to 24 months to work through the economy.

At this stage, the plight of the defendants would look distinctly shaky. After all, since 1972 the Chancellor allowed the money stock to increase by more than 20 per cent a year and yet was taken by surprise 18 months later when inflation started escalating beyond 10 per cent. Indeed, the three leading exponents of the gamble on growth can be shown by copious quotations to have gone on denying the danger signals up to December when the oil crisis gave them a temporary alibi for all that has followed.

'Classic Symptoms of Inflation'

By the autumn all the classic symptoms of inflation were plainly visible. Abroad, there was the sinking pound (which, please note, *raised* the sterling prices of imported raw materials, etc) and the record balance-of-payments deficit (which, pray ponder, *moderated* the domestic inflation by exporting excess purchasing power to our overseas suppliers). At home, witness after witness called attention to spreading shortages, unfilled vacancies, lengthening delivery dates, quickening pace of price increases, and other familiar evidence of over-heating.

Faced with the record, and remembering he is under oath, Mr Heath might go for a strong plea of mitigation. Had not his motive been of the purest? Faced with statistical unemployment approaching the million mark and anxious to dodge the old 'stop-go', he decided to 'reflate' the economy in the hope that increased output would match the massive injection of purchasing power which culminated in a 'borrowing requirement' (i.e. over-spending) of £4,000 million in the Budget a year ago. Even when businessmen complained of labour shortages, Mr Heath remained mesmerised by the macro-statistics of unemployment. Hence, his oft-repeated grouse that the grand strategy for perpetual growth was being sabotaged by feeble industrialists who failed to expand output, investment and employment to keep ahead of inflation.

The significance of this line of defence is that Mr Heath's mis-judgement was shared by a large number of other accessories. For a start, Mr Wilson and his most vocal colleagues are immediately

36

removed from the spectators' gallery into the dock. After exaggerating unemployment in 1972, they had welcomed the 'commitment to growth' — as had a very long list of gullibles headed by Mr Campbell Adamson and the CBI, to say nothing of such other weather-vanes as Lord Vic Feather and the combined TUC, Sir Fred Catherwood and NEDC, the ever-expansionist NIESR, Andrew Shonfield, Roger Opie and endless participants in *The Money Programme* and similar TV phoney inquests. Little better can be said of most leader writers (including, alas, *The Economist*), Michael Stewart and other trendy authors of Penguin Specials, and similar hindsighted pundits now shaking their heads over the collapse of the umpteenth experiment in forced growth.

'Witnesses to Error'

Indeed, it is easier to single out the comparative handful of witnesses innocent of what Lord Robbins dignified as a 'crisis of intellectual error'. Among journalists, the most persistent warnings came from Graham Hutton, Paul Bareau, Samuel Brittan, Peter Jay (who wrote 'The boom that must go bust' last May), and Patrick Hutber, with the *Daily Telegraph*, the *Banker* and *The Spectator* keeping their heads. When one outstanding independent banker, Walter Salomon, repeated a year ago his urgent warnings against inflation as the 'arch-disintegrator of society', his book *One Man's View* was loftily ignored by *The Times* and *Financial Times*.

Among MPs the unwavering voice of Enoch Powell was echoed audibly only by Nicholas Ridley and a handful of Tories with some muted mutterings on the Labour benches. Among professional economists, a relatively small if growing number mostly associated with the Institute of Economic Affairs and the Economic Research Council have maintained a spirited campaign against monetary excesses, led by such outstanding champions as Alan Walters, Gordon Pepper and Harry Johnson.

When so few appear wholly exempt from blame and so many (including all three party leaders) seem still to need to learn the full error of their ways, the detached observer is bound to search deeper for the tainted source of 'intellectual error' which appears no less rampant among the Treasury knights than among the Oxbridge peers (Balogh and Kahn).

37

The trail would lead us back to the followers of Keynes who taught that governments could always mop up unemployment by 'fine-tuning' the economy and failed to see that insofar as the unemployed are immobile, have the wrong skills, live in the wrong place, insist through monopoly trade unions on uneconomic wages, or are better-off 'resting' between jobs, then increased monetary demand will drive up prices more surely than it will draw idle resources into production.

'Confusers of Counsels'

Confusers of counsels include the whole tribe of so-called 'labour economists' led by Hugh Clegg who have mostly shrunk from exposing the rigidities and restrictions of trade unions or the mechanism by which monopoly wage bargaining can price workers and firms out of business — unless governments obligingly float them off on a tide of rising inflation. Their sins of omission were inflamed by leader writers who beat their breasts about 'a million on the dole' when the IEA's *How Much Unemployment?* would have shown Mr Heath that it was largely a phantom army which could not be conscripted by old-fashioned Keynesian-type monetary expansion.

With so many guilty men, a strong plea for mercy might temper the verdict on the Conservative inflationists to a suspended sentence. Next week I shall review some of the far-reaching changes necessary to put an end to inflation. And you, dear reader, will have to judge what relevance the three parties' policies have to this central issue for the stability of our economy and society.

10
Who will save us?

The Spectator, 2 March 1974

FOR all who have grasped the fundamental monetary nature of inflation, the economic issue at this election is not the price of milk, mortgages or mousetraps but the general, continuing and accelerating debasement in the value of the £ at home and abroad. That debasement has followed the record growth in the money supply of between 20 and 30 per cent a year since Mr Heath took charge in 1970.

What is it that tempts so many politicians to play with the fire of inflation? The plain answer is that monetary expansion appears to offer a soft option by which governments can dodge awkward choices between unemployment and alternative ways of improving the working of a free economy in the face of obstruction from trade unions.

At the heart of the economic problem is the inescapable condition of limited resources against which competing demands are exerted by the sectional interests of unions, farmers, firms, regions, government departments, for the rival claims of consumption, investment, exports, welfare. In an environment of stable money, the division of incomes (i.e. claims over resources) is settled in however rough and ready a way by changes in relative market prices.

The unwelcome consequence is that if the general price level is held stable by monetary restraint, some prices (including wages as the price of labour) will rise less than others and may not rise at all, or may even fall in declining trades. Changes in relative prices call for adjustments which are particularly disturbing in a pampered, rigid economy where immobile labour, restrictive practices, dying ducks, subsidised stay-putters, and what Professor W. H. Hutt calls the 'strike-threat system' impair the responsiveness of labour and capital to the very shifts in demand and supply on which progress depends.

How much easier — in the short run — for government to squirt money around the economy and foster the illusion that everyone can get more without anyone having to move or get less; that all workers irrespective of skills or location can enjoy full employment without moderating their wage demands; that all firms can be kept in business without earning their own keep; and that the party men can spend more without the voters spending less.

Alas, after a brief boom while stocks and idle capacity are used up, reality reasserts itself with a vengeance. Inflated demand sucks in more imports, frustrates exports, sinks the floating pound, drives domestic prices higher and — witness the miners — sharpens the very conflicts which it was the dream of expansionists to banish.

'A Paralysis of the Pricing System'

So far from solving the problem, reliance on incomes policy first diverts attention from the true cause of inflation while things get worse and then spreads a paralysis of the pricing system on which our eventual hope of an efficient adjustment mechanism — as well as our freedom — must rely. As Professor C. J. Grayson, head of the Price Commission under Nixon's Phase 2, recently warned businessmen (no less than labour leaders and politicians), we are simply 'building our own cages' and have no escape except to 'get back to the competitive market system'.

Because of the delayed-action effect of monetary expansion, we have yet to reap the harvest of past excess which indicates a fall in the value of money nearer 20 per cent in 1974 than the 10 per cent of the recent past. In that case, whatever Mr Heath cooks up with building societies, interest rates must go still higher if the saver is to be left with a margin above the fall in value of his money and the tax on 'unearned' income.

Clearly, the sooner we stop inflating the money supply the sooner the fever will subside. Faced with a devil's brew of escalating demand and declining real output, the urgent desideratum remains for a large reduction in the budget deficit. Since taxes, whether on goods or take-home-pay, already inflame the symptoms of inflation, the most effective way for government to live within its income without resort to the printing press is by cutting expenditure.

Economies are anyway long overdue in such bloated spending as the capital projects of public authorities, the enfeebling subsidies to nationalised and private industry, the spawning bureaucracies, and the

---

Ralph Harris's Note for the Guidance of Unhappy Voters

Confronted with the choice of voting for nondescript nominees of Labour or Conservative parties, you may not relish your handiwork being brandished like a political scalp by Mr Wilson or Mr Heath as a statistic in favour or against the miners, the Common Market, incomes policy, high taxation, socialism, or 'conservatism', or either of the party leaders.

If you, nevertheless, wish to vote rather than abstain or spoil your paper, you may mark your cross against the least objectionable candidate and add a message to let him know what you really think on this or that — or of him or his leader.

So long as the 'intention is clear', your ballot paper will be sorted out on the night among a pile of 'doubtfuls'. It will then be shown by the presiding officer to all the candidates who are invited to adjudicate whether 'the intention is clear'. So long as your cross is marked against one name, the candidate claiming your vote is obliged to read your message publicly. After this salutary process, the winner is likely to be less cavalier in boasting of a triumphant vote of confidence in his party's policy or his leader's wretched record.

---

misplaced generosity of indiscriminate welfare in cash and kind. In a forthcoming book from Churchill Press ominously entitled *Must History Repeat Itself?*, Mr Antony Fisher concludes with a 10-year programme that could bring income tax down to 15 per cent, with no surtax, capital gains tax or VAT.

Removing Strikers' Privileges

To ease the withdrawal symptoms from inflation and assist the processes of adjustment, the monopoly power of unions must be prevented from pushing wages so high that a large number of workers and firms are left stranded once the Chancellor refuses to float them off on a rising tide of monetary inflation. The present picketing by miners of docks and power stations, however apparently 'peaceful', points to the critical reform. Strikers should lose their privileged exemption from the ordinary law on conspiracy which now enables them collectively in furtherance of an industrial dispute to inflict damage in ways that would be illegal if done by other groups or by individuals acting alone.

I can hear a chorus from shrill treble to growling bass objecting that resolute action to clip public spending and curb labour monopolies is 'politically impossible' and I concede it is not on the horizon of the three party manifestoes. But 12 per cent inflation, a statutory incomes policy and a three-day week were not in Mr Heath's prospectus in 1970, any more than devaluation, prescription charges and 'In Place of Strife' featured in Mr Wilson's euphoric pledges of 1964.

To judge from the mostly business-as-usual electioneering we have been witnessing, it is impossible to see any early escape from our present 'cage' of unavailing and crippling controls under either Mr Heath or Mr Wilson. Things will have to get worse before minds are concentrated on the fundamental redirection of economic policy based on monetary and competitive disciplines.

If you take the view that the sooner the rude awakening comes the quicker the reconstruction will start, you might grit your teeth and vote Labour for an early convulsion. Likewise, if you think the Conservatives will relearn their lessons better in opposition, you can bite the bullet and let Labour ruin things for a while — if they started their taxation/nationalisation nonsense, it would last a matter of months, not years.

On a dispassionate review, the only ground for positively supporting Mr Heath is if you think him sufficiently practised at somersaulting to turn back on such indelibly *dirigiste* and damaging policies as pay and price incantations, Wedgwood-Walker industrial tinkering, Willie Whitewash's compromising, corporativist, consensus consultations with the weary worthies of the TUC, CBI, NEDO, NFU, *et mon oncle EEC aussi*.

Of course, you should not be doctrinaire in voting against Conservatives. Indeed, there are some I would welcome the chance of supporting such as Boyson, Biffen, Body, Bell, Bruce-Gardyne, Du Cann, Deedes, Dykes, Eyres, Hall (Joan), Lamont, Lawson, Finsberg, Griffiths (Brian), Ridley, Moate, Marten, Thatcher, Proudfoot, Spicer (on approval), Benyon (the white hope of Huyton), and Howe (the last hope of salvation).

On Labour, etc. candidates it would be combining business with pleasure for me to vote for Jenkins (Roy), Prentice, Pardoe, Williams (Shirley), Walden, Maxwell, Fletcher, Houghton, Taverne, Foot (mouth and all), Grayson (Bristol SE) and Hargrave (Sidcup).

Who else then will save us? Our surest hope is that we will save ourselves as soon as we can be set free from the palsied, paralysing grip of the puny party pontiffs.

11

Like it or not, our society is based on the theory of capitalism

'Do those most eagerly seeking to deprive others of "privileges" set an example by adopting a simple life-style or do they appear to thrive on the trappings of power?'

The Times, 4 December 1974

THE health and vigour of a mature political democracy must depend on unhindered debate between opposing philosophies. This process is imperilled if the scales are tilted so far one way that it becomes difficult to win a hearing for the broad concept of liberal capitalism that has been sustained by some of the finest minds of this century: Keynes, Mises, Popper, Robbins, Hayek, Friedman. . . .

Yet we are in danger of reaching a point where intellectual discourse is sterilised by populist slogans and scolding. Even leading 'capitalists' are infected with an enfeebling guilt complex that makes them almost willing accomplices in the destruction of free markets which (as Bernard Levin warned last month) are the foundation of other freedoms: the right to vote — or even to strike.

No attack on economic freedom has proved more corrosive than the spread of the notion that its material superiority is fatally flawed by its moral inferiority to a centrally directed, statist economy. Wilhelm Röpke, the Christian author of *The Humane Economy* and tenacious critic of national socialism, used to say that, even if capitalism were not the best engine of material welfare, it would still merit our highest allegiance as the most moral social order available to fallen man. So I agree with Raymond Fletcher that the grand debate should start from the ethical credentials of alternative economic arrangements.

Even individuals who strive after the highest standards of moral conduct are moved by a complex mixture of motives. Adam Smith, who wrote *The Theory of Moral Sentiments* before *The Wealth of Nations*, thought that the most pervasive driving force in economic life was 'the effort of every man to better his condition'. This concept explains the stricture that 'capitalism' panders to selfishness, when what is meant is that individuals will exert themselves most keenly to advance the welfare of family, friends, locality, clubs, church or any other cause about which they care.

Some may wish it otherwise; but 'Man is very far gone from original righteousness', as the Prayer Book reminds us and I suspect most Jews, Humanists and Don't Knows will recognise the self-serving weakness of their own nature.

Which social/economic system provides the most fitting environment for man *as he now is* to live out his daily life and labour? Which system will function tolerably despite human frailty and fallibility? Does the fallen nature of man best accord with an open order of dispersed initiative which creates cohesion and harmony by harnessing self-interest through a direct link between effort and reward to achieve voluntary co-operation in production and exchange? Or should we applaud the collectivist vision which repudiates self-interest and elevates social goals that can be procured at the cost of private choices only by increasingly coercive central commands.

Liberal Capitalism, Law and Philanthropy

Certainly, 'capitalism', like nature itself, favours the strong and fleet of foot, but the demonology of *laisser faire* has not stopped societies resting on economic freedom from using taxation to help the halt and lame. Liberal capitalism does not operate in a vacuum but within a framework of law, enriched in the West by philanthropy, voluntary societies, civic pride, individual example. ... If — in Alfred Marshall's dichotomy — it appeals to the strongest motives, it leaves ample scope for the highest.

Yet, because what Samuel Brittan has called 'the corrected market economy' puts a high value on freedom for consumers and so for producers, it confines governmental coercion to specific *public goods* not amenable to competitive supply. National defence, internal law and order, standards of safety, honest weights and measures (including money) and government guarantee of basic needs — in cash or kind — go back beyond Beveridge or Lloyd George to the first Elizabethans.

In contrast, the approach favoured increasingly by all three parties since the war gives priority to collective consumption, uniformity, equality — even where human conditions differ. It extends the range of public goods by enforcing 'social objectives' in the production and distribution of an indefinitely extensible list of everyday personal goods and services. Economic freedom is consistent with prescribing a minimum standard of education, medical care, pensions, housing; collectivism drives on towards a monopoly of state provision outlawing private effort, preference and supply.

If human nature were immaculate, social goals would establish themselves more or less spontaneously. If we were not 'all socialists now' we would at least be fit to dwell in a collectivist paradise without the tensions, temptations and torments caused by frustrated private purpose. As it is, collectivism must apply increasing coercion to override individual striving and keep wayward man on the prescribed straight and narrow. That is why the further we depart from a recognisable 'capitalism', the faster we slide towards authoritarianism.

Morality and Choice

Moral growth for individuals springs from the exercise of choice. There is no moral merit in 'doing good' at gun-point. Merciless taxation — rising to 98 per cent on private income — blesses neither giver nor taker: it leaves the victim with the choice of acquiescing in legalised theft, fiddling his tax returns or fleeing while he may. Thus the denial of economic freedom induces schizophrenia or corrupts the governed. But does it foster virtue among the governors? If there are not enough saints to form a cabinet, let alone supply the armies to enforce its commands, how can we expect the politicians in charge to serve the 'public interest' instead of feathering their nests? Do those most eagerly seeking power to deprive others of 'privileges' set an example by adopting a simple life-style? Or do they appear to thrive on the trappings of power?

Consider how corruption has already tarnished the selfless ideals of those who would centralise power for noble ends. Observe how politicians who in theory most recoil from the sordid play of self-interest, in practice promote a daily, deafening appeal to covetousness. In my lifetime it has been politicians describing themselves as 'socialists' or 'progressive conservatives' who — with few honourable exceptions like Sir Stafford Cripps — have more often led the field in promising voters *self*-enrichment at the expense of landlords, profiteers, speculators or some other convenient — even non-existent — minority. Beneath the moral-political crusade invariably dwells a careful, corrupting calculation about the short-term material self-interest of at least a working majority of the electorate.

The 'unacceptable face' of human nature is far worse in government than in business where competition and law can set limits to the harm that bad men will do. So I conclude that the avoidable excesses of the profit (and wage) maximisation incentive under economic freedom are as nothing compared to the incurable moral hazards of the vote-maximisation appeal by which collectivists entice us to surrender power to them. And for what end? We have 'castrated capitalism' in return for Pigou's mess of political potage which now threatens both individual freedom and national solvency.

12

Neddy for the knacker's yard

Ralph Harris finds the track record of the National Economic Development Council too harmful to justify running it again.

The Daily Telegraph, 17 November 1975

WITH the Government now talking about 'picking the winners' the question asks itself whether we should put any more of our money on Neddy in the economic recovery stakes. The National Economic Development Council, to give it its full dignity, is after all no promising yearling. It has been around a long time and the form book tells its own story.

Set up by Mr Selwyn Lloyd as Chancellor in 1961, the council was to provide a top level, semi-independent forum in which senior economic Ministers could consult with representatives of the CBI, TUC and nationalised industries. In euphoric phrases worthy of Mr Wilson, Neddy was to 'formulate broad national objectives' aimed at 'securing and controlling sustained expansion' by an approach which 'can be characterised as a changeover from the static to the dynamic which, because of its concern with growth, has added a time dimension to policy-making'. There were always plenty of words, but what of its works?

In the bad old days before Neddy tried to transform Britain's economy, the balance of payments generally ran a current surplus measured in hundreds of millions of pounds (compared with today's deficit in billions); unemployment ranged between 250,000 and 500,000 (now well over a million); national output rose annually between 2 and 3 per cent (at present falling); prices increased by 3 or 4 per cent a year (now 25 to 30 per cent).

48

Clearly, 14 years and two devaluations later, Neddy cannot be credited with having helped. But should we give the old nag another chance to prove its paces under ringmaster Dennis Healey? Before putting what's left of our shirt on Neddy, we should pause to ask whether its past failures were due to bad luck or whether they follow from the nature of the beast.

'By Consensus Out of Frustration'

In the parlance of the turf, Neddy was sired by consensus out of frustration. In the 1950s Britain's economic performance lagged behind France and Germany, but every time Chancellors tried to 'go for growth' the rise in wages and prices pushed the balance of payments into deficit, brought the pound under pressure and provoked credit squeezes which prompted complaints about the 'go-stop' cycle. If only we could increase our growth rate, the circular argument ran, higher output would take care of everything: exports, investment, consumption, Government spending could all go merrily ahead without inflation.

It was to square this circle that Neddy launched into what was then all the rage in the form of French-style 'indicative planning'. In a highly impressive statistical report entitled 'Growth of the UK Economy to 1966' it argued that the growth in output could be lifted from its previous level of 2·7 to 4 per cent a year provided all concerned — Government, management, employees — put their shoulders to the national wheel.

Brave new words were endlessly coined to express the consensus. Neddy's planning was to be 'consultative', 'purposive', 'coherent' and 'comprehensive'. The Neddy Council smugly commended its programme as 'a new departure', while its first Director boasted of a 'major revolution in attitudes'. Journalists took it all very seriously and outdid one another in rivalling the *Economist's* 'Loud cheers for Ned'.

The dismal outcome hardly bears retelling. With Neddy's expert reassurance (in March 1964) that the balance of payment need not inhibit growth, Mr Reginald Maudling kept his foot on the accelerator. Yet before the end of 1964, it was the worsening balance-of-payments deficit that compelled the new Chancellor, Mr James Callaghan, to step on the brakes by raising Bank rate, squeezing credit and

49

inaugurating the familiar 'stop' phase of the cycle. In vain the new Labour Government sought to escape from reality by launching George Brown's National Plan into orbit — complete with Neddy's 'Statement of Intent' to check inflationary wage claims — only to acknowledge failure with the July freeze of 1966.

The epitaph on Neddy's fine hopes was the devaluation of the pound in 1967. So far from being ineffective, Neddy did positive damage by encouraging dreams of easy expansion. Its legacy can be inflation, which has made necessary the most severe contraction yet, thereby adding record unemployment to our witch's brew of inflationary recession.

The Cloven Hoof

'No recriminations', said Mr Wilson from the cosy Neddy re-union at Chequers the other day as he and his colleagues sought to resurrect the corpse with novel incantations about 'common strategy', 'involvement', 'participation', 'turning point', 'rolling plans'. The music changes but the ballyhoo lingers on ...

Is this 'new initiative' likely to prove any more successful? As Mr Wilson's old ally Aneurin Bevan used to say, why consult the crystal ball when you can look up the book?

The fatal fumblings of Neddy were not due to clumsy fingers but to its cloven hoof. However dressed up, the interventionist-planning approach is founded on a false diagnosis which leads unerringly to a wrong prescription. The essential *non sequitur* is that because competitive markets work imperfectly, politicised markets will work better.

Thus the latest talk from Neddy was all about 'identifying' particular 'sectors', 'sub-sectors', 'individual firms' for special support. But who will do it — and how? There was not a glimmer of the need for a general pervasive mechanism to enforce the efficient use of resources and keep all the multifarious parts of a complex economy working in step with the changing forces of supply and demand. Enoch Powell once likened competitive markets to computers which digest daily countless millions of facts, mostly unknown (and unknowable) to any central planners, and which emit price and profit signals for the guidance of consumers, producers, exporters, importers, savers, investors.

'Massive Incubus of Distortion'

Can it be imagined that a Neddy, ridden uneasily by TUC-CBI-Government, could ever tackle the real job of purging the mixed-up economy of the massive incubus of political distortion through taxation, price control, inflation, rent restriction, subsidies, nationalised monopolies, and all the rest? It was because the Neddy method relies on *ad hoc* intervention and endless exhortation that I charged it in the early days with substituting a hand-and-mouth-operated economy for the impersonal computer of competitive markets.

Rather than undo the mischief of past interferences, Neddy will be drawn on to add further absurdities in the hope of neutralising their worst effects. Instead of sweeping away price control which brings firms to the brink of bankruptcy, Neddy will rattle the begging bowl for Government relief — which might be forthcoming on condition that what's left of private industry does as it's told.

Whatever the last-ditch hopes of hard-pressed businessmen, I profoundly believe the CBI should take no further part in the charade. It after all shares enough blame for its part in Neddy's past failures. Let it, at least for a start, withdraw until the Government has struck from its wrists and feet the shackles of price control and excessive taxation both on its employees and on such profits as are left by inflation.

Perhaps it will take one more disastrous flutter before the Government and unions awaken to the plain truth that Neddy is the living embodiment of the mule, without pride of ancestry or hope of progeny. Until it is carted off to the knacker's yard, there is not much hope for revitalising Britain's over-burdened economy.

13

Freedom without unemployment

Unemployment or inflation were once thought to be alternatives. Now they rise in harness. Ralph Harris, Director of the Institute of Economic Affairs, argues that monetary control must be combined with policies to prevent trade unions pricing members out of their jobs.

Crossbow, Summer 1977

IF politicians refuse to learn from economic analysis, they will be driven in the end to learn from the often costly errors of experience. I have frequently pointed out that the Heath Government could have avoided stoking up the biggest inflation in British history if leading Ministers had read Milton Friedman's Wincott Lecture delivered a few months after they took office in June 1970. Entitled *The Counter-Revolution in Monetary Policy*, the lecture drew on empirical studies of many countries over long periods of history to conclude:

> '. . . inflation is always and everywhere a monetary phenomenon in the sense that it is and can be produced only by a more rapid increase in the quantity of money than in output.'

How many billions of pounds of lost output and hundreds of thousands of unemployed might have been avoided if Chancellor Tony (now Lord) Barber and his Treasury advisers had grasped the point and refrained from the inflation of M3 in the early 1970s?

Painful Lessons

It was the painful lesson of experience — reinforced perhaps by the writings of his son-in-law Peter Jay — that prompted Prime Minister Callaghan to relearn the truth which he told the Labour Party Conference in October 1976 as follows:

> 'We used to think that you could spend your way out of a recession and increase employment by cutting taxes and boosting government spending. I tell you that that option no longer exists, and that insofar as it ever did exist, it only worked by injecting bigger doses of inflation into the economy followed by higher levels of unemployment as the next step. That is the history of the past twenty years.'

The enormous cost we are now paying for the wrong-headed pursuit of full employment through monetary excess might yet prove a good bargain if we truly learn from this example of Tory/Labour/Treasury/NIESR/Bank of England/Cambridge folly.

Perhaps the first lesson is that the existence of a consensus is far from proving that the favoured idea is necessarily right. Indeed, when we recall all those panaceas backed by the post-war economic establishment — from NEDC and National Plan to EEC and incomes policy — it might seem sensible to start from the probability that anything about which there is agreement between the TUC, CBI, Treasury, NIESR, Balogh-Kaldor axis must be wrong. Thus today we might be on guard that all would certainly agree that the nationalised industries are here to stay and the welfare state cannot be dismantled. Might they not be proved wrong again?

But returning to inflation; what are the lessons we could learn that would make the terrible experience worth having endured? The first I would express more precisely than Mr Callaghan along the following lines: when the 'full employment' target is set above the equilibrium level consistent with stable prices, the result is *unnecessarily high unemployment* as well as *mounting inflation*. The importance of my formulation is that it directs attention to the best method of tackling these two evils that were once thought alternatives and have become twin torments.

Unemployment

If we ask how we can raise the equilibrium level of employment without inflation, we are driven back to ask what determines the safe level of unemployment — what Friedman calls the 'natural rate'. The short answer is: anything that obstructs the occupational or geographical matching of unemployed people with unfilled vacancies. At once attention is redirected to impediments and frictions that have nothing to do with increased monetary demand. One obvious example is the immobility of labour induced by rent control and subsidised council houses. Another is the national uniformity of wages and salaries in both public and private sectors which prices labour out of jobs that could be made available in less favoured areas. Above all, the major imperfection in the labour market is revealed as the monopoly power of trade unions.

It is a matter of elementary economic analysis that even the most entrenched monopolist cannot dictate both the price of its product or service and the amount it can sell. If it pitches the price too high, less will be bought and some part of supply will be left unsold. Thus we can explain inflation as the result of the government's effort to restore the full employment of over-priced labour by stimulating monetary demand through the Keynesian mechanism of budget deficits. Once monopoly unions take account of the resulting inflation by pushing their wage demands still further ahead of the marginal (current) value of output, government can try to maintain their full employment target only through speeding up the monetary inflation. In effect, it reduces the value of the money in terms of which higher wages are paid.

New Policy

The importance of this diagnosis is that it points to a prescription quite different from — and almost the precise opposite to — the policies Mr Callaghan inherited from Harold Wilson. It is true that since 1974, Mr Healey has somewhat erratically tried to get hold of the money supply and moderate the rate of increase below the record levels permitted under Mr Heath. But as theory tells us, the inevitable transitional effect is an increase in unemployment as the government refuses to supply the additional monetary demand that would be necessary to bring over-priced labour back into employment.

But a Labour Government built up on the historic foundation of the trade union movement has found it impossible to admit it is the pressure of these very labour monopolies that has brought the equilibrium level of employment so far below the oft-proclaimed target of full employment. If Mr Callaghan acknowledged that simple analytical insight, he would logically have to concede that the only way to combine monetary stability with higher levels of employment is to curb the monopoly power of trade unions to impose wage increases that price their members out of jobs. The appropriate policies would then be seen as making unions compatible with competitive market wages by attacking such monopoly devices as closed shop, blacking, boycotting, oppressive picketing and the subsidisation of strikes through social security and tax repayments.

Weakness

Of course, the Government's policies have been in the diametrically opposite direction of still further entrenching the monopoly power of unions — and then begging their leaders not to throw their weight about. In short, instead of tackling the institutional and legal impediments to a more freely competitive market — which could reduce the friction of unemployment without resort to inflation — recent policies have reduced freedom and flexibility still further. Thus as a price for imposing stricter monetary policy to reduce inflation, the Government has conceded trade unions additional power to increase unemployment. And in the process it has, in the name of the social contract, imposed higher taxes and more punitive controls over prices and profits that severely threaten freedom and can only weaken the economy's recuperative ability to extend viable employment.

The dearly-bought lessons from Tory/Labour post-war economic mismanagement, therefore, run far wider than the obvious and accepted need for monetary prudence. The most generally applicable lesson is that major economic disorders flow from impediments to the operation of the competitive market. Those disorders will not be remedied but aggravated by adding further impediments to the freedom and responsibility of employers and employees to strike mutually beneficial bargains on payment and productivity as the foundation of a high and stable level of employment. This is the lesson that most Conservative spokesmen show little sign of having learned. Until they do, we shall continue to pay the price in higher unemployment and diminished freedom.

14

The protection rackets

*Ralph Harris attacks a system which aids
inefficient producers at the customers' expense.*

The Daily Telegraph, 23 November 1981

BEWARE of economists. They are not always right. They often disagree with one another — and with themselves. All the more striking, therefore, is their consistent support over two centuries for the proposition that freedom of international trade advances the economic welfare of all participants.

The play of competitive markets is not like poker, where winners gain at the expense of losers. All trade is what the textbooks call 'a positive sum game' in which buyers and sellers join because *both* finish up better off than if they tried to be self-sufficient. The gain from trade in any particular case may be marginal, but the widening chain of domestic and international trade has transformed the efficiency with which every individual's labour or capital is applied.

Contrast the standard of living enjoyed in Britain or Hong Kong with the poverty of an isolated African or South American tribe. It is no exaggeration to say that all improvements in real income have followed the extension of trade from primitive barter between neighbouring families to the exchange of goods and services by individuals at opposite ends of the world.

Protectionism Damages Your Wealth

Protectionism, on the other hand, can seriously damage your wealth. The danger comes from the ease with which it can be dispensed for every economic malady under such reassuring labels as: employment tonic, foreign pest repellent, infant growth stimulant, geriatric reviver, strike soothing ointment, redundancy pain-killer pills and, of course, all-purpose tranquillisers. Once swallowed, increasing doses may become necessary.

The process that has already started, to fend off awkward adjustments in employment and investment, is in danger of being extended and perpetuated. The result would be that the body economic could no longer maintain present standards of living around the world, much less resume the improvement many have come to take for granted.

Such fears may seem remote. Yet in many countries nominally conservative, liberal or social-democrat governments are turning away from the post-war presumption in favour of free trade. Without the pretext of national defence or infant industries, they are improvising domestic subsidies and foreign quotas in such long-established industries as textiles, steel, motor cars. They have been increasingly led to protect particular incomes and maintain employment against disturbance due to market changes in supply and demand.

It is to this political search for security that we can trace the malignant infection of protectionism at home and abroad. The simple truth is that all economic progress depends on shifting capital and labour into new products, methods, locations. Every invention which ends up benefiting the consumer starts off by hurting the producers of whatever it supplants.

The strongest pressure on government is, therefore, to protect entrenched producers against the dispersed interest of consumers. Though some producers appear to benefit in the short run, everyone stands to lose in the end. The favoured gain not only at the expense of foreign competitors but also of domestic consumers and workers in exporting industries, or, in the case of subsidies, at the expense of the taxpayers.

What we are again witnessing is the age-old battle between the conflicting requirements of social security and economic progress. By intervening to protect particular incomes and employments, government frustrates the process of adaptation to change.

Political Intervention Disrupts Change

Politicians invariably excuse their interventions as 'temporary measures' to ease the path of change. More often the result is to replace prompt, gradual and continuing adjustment to market forces by delayed and discontinuous disruption through the contentious political process. The danger we see around the world is that by further weakening the incentives for producers to adjust, protectionism reinforces the already powerful anti-market forces making for rigidity, immobility, instability and economic stagnation. While it is always possible for a single country to benefit by checking imports that compete with domestic production, once other countries play this game it becomes self-defeating.

Protectionism is thus a costly form of economic warfare that impoverishes all and cannot be relied on to afford security. The solution is all-round economic disarmament, each country agreeing not to use economic weapons it does not relish having used against it. In 1947 the General Agreement on Tariffs and Trade was established to conduct and police such mutually beneficial agreements. GATT stood then as it stands today for the proposition that the national interest of all countries is served by an open international order of free trade based on clear rules that limit government meddling with the market.

It may be asked: if a government abides by GATT does it not lose part of its own sovereignty? The answer is that all governments do sacrifice some power — the anarchic power to hurt one another and damage themselves — but they also gain or regain an important source of power, the GATT-given power to resist the pressure of domestic vested interests and to transmit the discipline of competitive markets from international trade to national industry.

Reversing Decades of Protection

Britain's relative decline over the past century illustrates the folly of seeking security by shielding from change. Mrs Thatcher's task can be summed up as reversing decades of protectionism resulting from increased subsidies, state welfare, nationalisation, trade unionism and so-called 'employment protection'. With the best of intentions weak government had allowed the economy to become rigid and resistant to the adjustments now made irresistible by such changes as advanced technology, expensive oil and new competition from developing countries, especially the market oases of Asia, including Hong Kong and Japan.

Mrs Thatcher's central strategy is to replace past weakness by strong, unyielding government — starting with monetary discipline — and so to impose flexibility, mobility and adjustment on the previously cosseted managements and workers of British industry. If Mrs Thatcher can hold her course, we will see a more competitive Britain earning its own security without the need for protectionism in its various disguises.

The only lasting cure is the tonic of the free-market economy. Milton Friedman has suggested a text which every entrepreneur should hang over his desk: 'If I knew for a certainty that a man was coming to my house with the conscious design of doing me good, I should run for my life'. I will add my favourite text: 'No man's life, liberty or property are safe while the legislature is in session'.

And that goes, alas, even for the House of Lords.

15

What about the workers?

Ralph Harris examines the facts behind the three million unemployed and suggests a free market in jobs is their best hope.

The Daily Telegraph, 17 March 1982

JUST as after 1945 there was too much optimism about full employment, there is now too much pessimism about unemployment. If economists had stuck to their last, as my old teacher Sir Dennis Robertson used to urge, they would always have insisted that the political slogan of full employment was a mirage. In a world of ceaseless change in techniques, demand and foreign trade, there is no way of guaranteeing old jobs in declining areas nor of shifting people instantly into new work developing elsewhere.

The traditional economists knew better when they distinguished such categories as frictional, structural and cyclical unemployment. The length of time people were out of work between jobs was then understood to depend on the occupational and geographical mobility of labour in adapting to new opportunities.

Among the worst obstacles have been council housing, which made people reluctant to move homes, and the antique system of trade union apprenticeships which prevented people acquiring new skills in mid-career.

To the unemployment inevitably arising from such inflexibility in the labour force, must be added the avoidable loss of jobs due to pushing wage costs above the value of output. Here trade union industrial and political power is the main culprit. This industrial power is deployed to impose restrictive practices that reduce output per man and simultaneously to extract unearned wage increases that raise unit costs.

Union political power has been exerted to saddle industry with welfare policies that now account for over a quarter of total labour costs. The resulting rise in British costs and prices has added to unemployment both by pricing our staple exports (e.g. ships) out of overseas markets and losing domestic trade (e.g. cars) to foreign imports.

No Penalty for Appeasement

A fair question is why British industry did not make a firmer stand against trade union restrictions and higher wages? The short answer is that as long as governments were committed to full employment the penalty for appeasement was not very pressing.

Until the 1970s, both Labour and Tory governments acted on simple-minded Keynesian lines to meet any threat of rising unemployment by increasing public spending or reducing taxes to stimulate demand so as to restore full employment.

So businessmen thought they had little to fear from yielding to trade union pressure. If they conceded excessive wages, the Chancellor would boost the general level of demand and they could hope to pass on higher costs in higher prices. Increasingly, the effect of increased spending was less and less to raise the demand for unemployed labour and more and more to finance the rise in costs and prices.

In the recent Hobart Paper* the authors Robert Miller and John Wood have a revealing table that shows the cost of accommodating union wage grab.

Thus in the four Macmillan years 1958-62 the effect of increasing total spending by 25 per cent was split roughly equally in raising output by 12·7 per cent and pushing prices up by 12·2 per cent. In the four Wilson-Callaghan years 1974-78 an increase in total spending of almost 100 per cent financed a derisory increase in output of 8 per cent and a rise in prices of over 90 per cent.

And let Mr Peter Shore take note, this massive increase in spending did not stop unemployment doubling from under 700,000 in 1974 to around 1,400,000 in 1978.

If rising inflation was bad for employment, the effect of slowing it

* *What Price Unemployment?*, IEA, price £1.80.

down must make unemployment for a while even worse. Thus businessmen had got into the habit of allowing costs to rise in the expectation that the Government would provide the extra money to accommodate the resulting higher prices for their products.

The effect of Mrs Thatcher's refusal to finance increasing inflation is to return responsibility for employment to businessmen and their workers. Either they break the old habits and between them curb costs so as to survive as inflation comes down, or they price themselves out of markets at home and abroad, with predictable effects on bankruptcies and unemployment.

After decades of weak governments it was difficult in 1979 to believe that Mrs Thatcher's economic ministers would stand firm. Spurred on by Clegg, wages rose in the first year by between 20 per cent and 30 per cent. Since the Chancellor was not going to finance a similar escalation of inflation, only two outcomes were left. Either managements had to squeeze labour costs (which make up 90 per cent of total value added) to stay in business or they went to the wall.

Although both responses in the short run increased unemployment, wherever the efficiency road was taken it has led to often dramatic improvements in the competitiveness of British businesses.

The cost in lost jobs would have been less but for the appalling burden of local rates (60 per cent of which fall on business) and the unchecked price increases of nationalised industries which are sheltered from the discipline of competition.

The clear lesson of this Hobart Paper is that employment can be analysed in a market — like that for petrol or smoked salmon — where both supply and demand are influenced by price. Unfortunately, at the same time as demand for labour has been reduced by its high price, the supply has been discouraged by whittling away the incentive of many people to work for highly taxed wages rather than to settle for generous, untaxed social benefits.

Better Off On the Dole

Messrs Miller and Wood show that hundreds of thousands of family men are better off unemployed — even without taking account of the pickings available in what is variously called the informal, underground, hidden or black economy.

Grievous though high unemployment may be as the price of past folly by governments and trade unions, this Paper explains that the much-advertised three million are not to be thought of as an ever-lengthening queue of workless.

Even in 1980 there were over eight million changes of jobs, so that on average each month over 600,000 were taken into work. The trouble has been that a still larger number have lost their jobs. But that does not have to go on.

If we want the labour market to work better to raise demand for workers and encourage supply, the analysis points to a whole variety of measures that could help.

First, anything more Mr Norman Tebbit can do to weaken the obstructive power of trade unions will speed the return to realistic wages and working practices.

Second, the relative attractions of living on welfare would be reduced if the promised taxation of unemployment benefits was matched by lower taxes on earnings.

Third, Wages Councils and other protective measures that raise the cost of employing people, especially the young, should be abolished.

Abolish Rent Control for Mobility

Fourth, the abolition of rent control could bring a million or more empty houses onto the market to ease mobility of labour. And, of course, anything that improves the efficiency of nationalised industry would help by reducing prices and taxes.

Above all, it is no use looking to posturing politicians to tell us where future jobs will come from. If Mr Peter Shore had been told in 1950 that half a million workers were *permanently* to lose their jobs in agriculture, do you suppose he would have known that two million new jobs were going to be found in one single category of professional services?

If we remove present obstacles, I have no doubt the market will provide as many jobs as the producing population are willing to take — at prices the consuming population is prepared to pay.

16

Don't just polish — abolish

The Times, 24 August 1983

ASIDE from its success against inflation, Mrs Thatcher's government has made disappointing progress in restoring vigour to the economy. A start has been made with denationalisation and trade union reform, but state spending has not been cut, local government is as big as ever and little has been done to free the labour market or to move welfare policy from universal provision to help for those in need.

I do not believe that, whatever the International Labour Organisation's objections, we could not get rid of wages councils, which set minimum rates for almost three million people, mostly in retailing — 60 per cent of the adult rate at 16, against 20 per cent in Switzerland — and which gravely damage youth employment prospects.

It seems strange that a government which professes to support a market economy should not have taken positive action against impediments that raise unit labour costs (employment protection, national insurance, trade union restrictive practices); that obstruct mobility (rent control, regional development, council house subsidies) or that reduce take-home pay (high taxes on low earnings) to little, if anything, above social benefits.

In most cases, the Government has not changed its policies. It has been diverted from its objectives by legislature and bureaucratic obstruction.

'An Insatiable Appetite for Legislation'

Modern government is appallingly complex and has an insatiable appetite for legislation. In a single recent year, 70 new Acts of Parliament and 2,000 'statutory instruments' were spewed over 6,000 printed pages. Here is a major source of power for civil servants who can blind even the brightest ministers with almost incomprehensible legalistic jargon in which they, as narrow specialists, are always more expert.

Suppose a company had to get approval for amending its articles of association every time it wanted to change a price, alter a product, withdraw a service, borrow money or make any one of hundreds of day-to-day adjustments to its operations. Imagine the staff it would need, the delay and distraction leading to virtual paralysis.

Yet we would all agree that bureaucrats cannot be allowed the range of discretion in dispensing state resources and authority that businessmen enjoy in balancing the interests of customers and shareholders. Because there is no government equivalent to the commercial price-profit system to keep civil servants in check, we have ceaseless legislative amendment and intolerable pressure on the parliamentary timetable to permit tardy adjustment to changing circumstances or a new government's policy.

These necessary restraints are so lethal to flexibility and change that government should be confined to the barest minimum of functions which it has to finance through taxation because a free market cannot provide them. The cumbersome processes of amendment and reforms should therefore take second place to outright repeal of unnecessary, obstructive statutes.

Like the Mikado's Lord High Executioner, the non-party repeal group in the House of Lords has 'a little list of society offenders that never would be missed'. In addition to the job-destroying wages councils, our targets include the restrictive Shops Act, the antique Truck Acts, the paternalistic licensing laws, such monopolies as the solicitors in conveyancing and opticians in selling spectacles, to say nothing of the Rent Acts that have shrunk the housing market and still impede the mobility of labour.

How to Reduce Taxation

We are left with the problem of reducing taxes as the golden route to reducing costs throughout the economy and sharpening incentives, especially for the lower paid to work rather than live off social benefits. To search out savings, we should examine every welfare and local government service now provided 'free' and ask why most people should not choose and pay through direct fees and insurance rather than indirectly through inflated taxes and rates. The way to help the poor is not to give everyone else free services but to top up low incomes and reduce everyone's taxes.

The aim should be to halve public expenditure and reduce total taxation to the safe limit of 25 per cent of national income. A subordinate aim is to restore politics to a part-time job suitable for gentlemen and lords, that is for unpaid amateurs who have to earn their living in the real world and pay their share of (lower) taxes like the rest of us.

17

Where aid is sown, poverty and debt are harvested

Ralph Harris argues that foreign aid hinders more than it helps.

The Independent, 1 October 1987

IT is hardly surprising that most people spontaneously support the idea of foreign aid. Who would not wish to help those starving figures from Africa, Asia and South America who periodically haunt our television screens? But emergency help for victims of drought or floods is quite distinct from annual subsidies to governments that are often directly responsible for the plight of their people.

Let us be clear. 'Foreign aid' has nothing to do with handing cash or food to individuals in need. It is a question-begging term to describe the continuing political transfer of funds between governments, originally intended to promote the long-term economic development of what used to be called 'backward countries'.

Despite having been tactfully rechristened Less Developed Countries, most of the recipients are still economically backward after 30 years of 'aid'. Their record mocks the earlier theory of 'take-off into self-sustaining growth'. The reality is that most 'aid' can be seen to have bolstered muddled/Marxist/militarist régimes that have little to show except poverty and debt for past political gifts and soft loans.

This failure of 'aid' to yield lasting economic development should direct attention to the lonely critique deployed by the former London School of Economics professor P. T. (now Lord) Bauer, author of many scholarly studies grounded in first-hand knowledge of what used to be called, hopefully, the 'developing world'.

For all their apparent differences, most recipients of 'aid' suffer from a common handicap. It is not lack of natural resources, which many have in abundance and which are not necessary for economic progress, as demonstrated by the remarkable advance of Hong Kong, Taiwan and even Japan.

Delusion of Central Planning

The common handicap is self-inflicted. It is the once-fashionable delusion that central economic planning is the only way forward. The costs which this fallacy has visited on more than half the world's population are almost impossible to exaggerate.

Professor Lord Bauer never tires of reciting the multifarious ways in which such governments have retarded agriculture and distorted industrial development. We have seen them embark on extensive price control, suppression of private trade, restrictive licensing, indiscriminate nationalisation, the setting up of marketing monopolies, manipulation of exchange rates and the prohibition of holding stocks in the name of preventing 'hoarding'.

In a Lords debate on starvation in the Third World, I ventured to pose the question: Why is the weather always so much worse in socialist countries? I quoted evidence from an American symposium on 'The Distortion of Agricultural Incentives' that wherever prices are free to fluctuate, peasants respond to economic inducements by increasing output, just as traders shift stocks from areas of surplus to areas of shortage. If only governments would discharge their primary function of ensuring security for person and property, peasants and traders would automatically store food to provide against bad times.

In the absence of secure property rights over their land, peasants indulge in casual, nomadic cultivation which leads to over-cropping, over-grazing and the destruction of ground cover. The result has been to increase soil erosion and convert fertile land into desert. When the world was shocked by pictures of famine in Ethiopia, the Marxist government was pursuing a 'co-operative' policy of annual re-allocation of plots, which positively discouraged good husbandry. Why should itinerant farmers bother to fertilise the land, improve drainage or clear boulders?

Further south in Tanzania, President Nyerere was bathing in the flattery of western 'progressives' for his vision of African socialism, which herded millions into collective farms that converted an exportable surplus of food production into a chronic deficit.

If the primary failure has been to retard agricultural development, it has been reinforced by obstructing profitable industry. There has been widespread persecution of multinational companies which were a major instrument for spreading training, employment and prosperity. Yet throughout Africa (apart from the South) their operations have been fettered: managements compulsorily replaced by local staff, remittances of profit restricted, and assets often seized without adequate compensation.

'Aid' Encourages White Elephants

At the same time, 'aid' has enabled the recipient governments to embark on political prestige projects such as lavish building of capital cities, running subsidised airlines and 'investment' in every kind of industrial white elephant. Most shameless of all is the massive spending on armaments. An official West German source estimated that the Third World accounts for one-fifth of all arms spending. It hardly needs to be said that most of the weapons are for use by rulers against their own people or other Third World countries.

This list far from exhausts the catalogue of economic crimes by most recipients of 'aid'. Leave aside the corruption practised by many rulers and copied lower down. Consider the way ruling factions have persecuted rival tribes and immigrant minorities who are often among the most enterprising and productive people in countries desperately short of both qualities. A seminal insight of Lord Bauer is that 'aid' strengthens the power of recipient governments and so intensifies the politicisation of economic and social life. The individual's welfare, even survival, may depend on the whim of politicians or their *apparatchiks*, thereby raising the stakes in the struggle for power.

The resulting tensions periodically erupt into armed conflict. More generally and invisibly, the damage is done by diverting the energies and resources of the most able and ambitious individuals away from productive economic activity into personal fulfilment through politics.

Apart from a few successful projects — which could have attracted commercial investment — 'aid' has not generally helped. Worse, it has more often hindered by providing incompetent governments with a soft option that has enabled them to delay putting their economic houses in order. It has bred a surly spirit of dependency made worse by the piling up of debts they cannot pay. Just ponder. If past loans had been invested as risk capital the burden of failure would have fallen on foreign equity investors, not on governments with nothing to show for the money. Above all, commercial investment would have been more likely to create lasting wealth, employment and prosperity.

18

An Easter offering to the bishops

The Sunday Telegraph, 3 April 1988

SINCE confession is good for the soul, let me say straightaway that some practical manifestations of private enterprise strike me as unalluring. Forty years' study of economics have weaned me from Beveridge and Keynes to advocate competitive enterprise as the nearest we have to a panacea in this imperfect world. But I'm never surprised that this view is resisted by some of the nicest people — as well as some of the other sort.

While most company chairmen I have got to know would be equally at home in a university common room, or even on a church committee, a few leave a lot to be desired. Does that mark them out from others? What about top politicians, trade union leaders, academics, playwrights, broadcasters, who compete for our favour? Are they not a pretty mixed bag? Come to that, dear reader, what about you?

On Easter Sunday we might all, including our bishops, agree that we fall well short of the Christian ideal of selfless devotion to others. Oh yes, on our good days all but the worst are capable of rare feats of generosity or self-sacrifice. But the best of us can be horribly insensitive to the feelings and well-being even of those we like or love. (Here, all but the Perfect Ones can join in saying Amen!)

Old Adam

Such Easter reflections on human nature go to the heart of our choice between alternative economic and social systems. At its simplest the economic problem resolves itself into a continuous battle over the use of scarce human and material resources. More for one means less for another unless ...? You've got it: unless human ingenuity goes on producing more for all by discovering new resources and increasing the efficiency with which they are used.

And how, pray, are we most likely to enlarge the supply of said scarce resources and economise in demand for them? By appealing to people as Perfect Ones who will always give of their best and never count the cost? Or by engaging their interests and making it worth their while to do their stuff by working, saving, investing, inventing and economising in competitive markets?

Adam Smith had no doubt about the answer. He is often mocked as the canny Scot who thought that inside every human being there was another Scotsman trying to get out.

Yet in his first treatise on *The Theory of Moral Sentiments*, he acknowledged the place of sympathy, fellow-feeling, benevolence and love in man's complex make-up. He warned, however, that such 'sublime' regard for others, 'can never be an excuse for his neglecting the more humble department . . . the care of his own happiness, of that of his family, his friends, his country'.

So before we can indulge our benevolent instincts, we need prudently to attend to our own affairs. Hence in his magnum opus entitled *An Enquiry into the Nature and Causes of the Wealth of Nations*, our Adam put his money on the 'uniform, constant and uninterrupted effort of every man to better his condition . . .' as the most dependable engine of economic progress.

Shallow critics have denounced this mainspring of human striving in the market-place as narrow 'self-interest', or even 'greed' and 'grab'. But in Smith's vision the free market economy allows the widest play for us all to pursue our *self-chosen* purposes. We are all free to try fulfilling our ideals by working for others at a pittance. But we might agree that Ford, Nuffield, Sainsbury, Marks & Spencer have done most good by maximising their earnings so as to give more generously to good causes.

To avoid the parrot-cry of *laissez-faire*, I must add that a free economy requires an indispensable role for strong (not big) government. It calls for a legal framework that guarantees the security of person and property, partly by policing contracts and preventing force and fraud. It also requires some form of state (as well as charitable) provision of cash (and counsel) for individuals who are unable by their own efforts 'to better their condition'.

Consenting Adults

Hayek has claimed that the highest merit of the market economy is in checking the evil bad men can wreak in the centralised societies we see around the world. In the economic battle over scarce resources, competition within the law is a peaceful and productive way of resolving conflicts between individuals and interest groups. Buying and selling between consenting adults is most likely to confer what economists call gains from trade on both parties.

The chief danger, for both the economy and democracy, is of people ganging together to escape from the rigours of competition by seeking subsidies and protection from pliant politicians. We live increasingly in a world of pressure groups, from farmers, trade unions, the professions and other monopoly mongers, to the mixed bag of 'welfare' lobbies.

So let me ask each reader this Sunday: What's your particular racket? Why not repent of looking to government for special favours and settle for the market on the principle: Do competitively as you would be done by?

And if any bishop reads these words, I beg him understand that the market is morally neutral. It responds to higher demands as readily as to grosser appetites. His job is by preaching, prayer and example to help elevate vulgar preferences.

When bishops blame the market for every excess, they are no better than the fat man in the restaurant who blames his own obesity on the waiter.

73

19

£50,000,000,000 is not enough?

The Sunday Telegraph, 10 April 1988

Aｌｅｒｔ readers will not have missed the recent contrast between this column's encouraging reflections on poverty and the earnest anxieties of my old friend Paul Barker about the losers from the Fowler reforms of social benefits.

I doubt whether anyone not paid to master the intricacies of income support (in place of supplementary benefits), family credits (in place of FIS), social fund (in place of single payments), housing benefits, and the rest can arrive at a confident verdict on how these changes will turn out.

Of course, we will hear more from the lobbies of losers (unemployed youths, better-off pensioners) than from the much larger number of gainers (disabled, single parents, low earner families, poorest pensioners).

Value for Money?

I certainly hold no brief for the details of the Fowler reforms, however well-intentioned their conception. They end marginal tax rates above 100 per cent on earnings, so that people are no longer worse off taking a job. But many will still face penal rates up to 95 per cent.

Let me repeat that there can be no tolerable solution to poverty and work incentives until the yoke of income tax is once and for all lifted from people on low incomes.

One proposition on which all might agree for a start is that the community should give highest priority — second only to wealth-creation — to helping those unable to help themselves. By that test this Government has failed, like its predecessors, to tackle the radical reshaping of spending, taxation, social and housing policies. That is

74

one reason we get such poor value from spending the staggering sum approaching £50,000,000,000 on social benefits.

But who can name any major Government programme that gives us good value for money? Why is it that throughout my life state provision always appears to give so much less satisfaction than private suppliers?

Look around: Read the papers. Watch television. Where are the problems? Do we find housewives demonstrating against super-markets, motorists besieging garages, handymen denouncing DIY centres, or paying-guests roughing-up hotel staff? Instead, the chief focus of discontent shifts back and forth between state schooling, council tower blocks, universities, local authority services, the NHS and now social benefits.

Why do so-called 'public' services, provided in the 'public interest' by 'public servants' at 'public' expense, so often fail to satisfy the poor old public? What is it about government that guarantees widespread dissatisfaction?

This is no party point. Bear in mind that throughout the post-war period something around half the national income has been spent, year in, year out, by both Labour and Conservative administrations. Recall all those confident election promises of remarkable solutions for every ill the flesh is heir to. With such a torrent of spending over four decades, should we not have swept away some of our problems?

Alas, there is no way we can ever get value for money from 'representative government' to compare with the value we get from self-government in the market-place.

It was Lionel Robbins who compared the competitive market to a perpetual referendum in which we all vote every day with our pennies and pounds. We choose between the widest conceivable range of goods and services supplied by myriad competing producers, each with a powerful incentive to meet our individual preferences and give value for money. However eccentric our tastes, there's likely to be a choice of suppliers.

In stark contrast, the political market offers us one vote between two or three brands every four or five years. Instead of item-by-item choice *à la carte*, each party manifesto offers a single *table d'hôte* menu on a take-it-or-leave-it basis. While competing market goods and services come in every shape and size marked with separate price tags, the rival packages of party policies are heavily wrapped in red or blue ribbons and are distinctly cagey on costs. (That's one reason people vote for more government than they really want to pay for.)

Respect for Minorities

Above all, the market-place caters for minority preferences in a way representative government can never match. Our ethnic minorities should be among the keenest champions of the market. They don't have to lobby or demonstrate to get what they want from competing suppliers. Indian shops and restaurants spring up, where Indian parents have no way of getting the schools they want for their children.

The enlargement throughout this century of the scale and scope of the state has led to the neglect by hard-pressed governments of their primary duties and the politicisation of more and more aspects of our lives. With the spread of politics we have seen the aggravation of conflict.

Take all the recent distasteful public debate about homosexuality in schools. Extreme bitterness is provoked by the use of state money to promote ideas which the majority does not like. If people must indulge their strange tastes, the general view would be that they should do so within the law, in private, and from private pockets.

In short, the market allows people to do their own thing at their own expense. By contrast, politicians before 1979 were always offering to do more things for us on the cheap. But as people tumble to the truth that political gifts come dear (and often shoddy) the revolt against bloated government will gather pace. Perhaps the Bishop of Durham should keep a few of his curses in reserve for use in those happier days.

20

Student loans are better than grants

The Sunday Telegraph, 24 April 1988

Drawing on an insight of Adam Smith, I am tempted to unveil a variant of Hutber's Law ('improvement means deterioration') that might be called the Hutber-Harris Law. It would state, more cautiously, that political good intentions, especially in giving away money, tend to have disappointing, if not disastrous, consequences.

This law could be illustrated from a variety of social policies where more spending has simply bought more trouble. My chosen example to launch it is from the elevated world of universities.

Have you notice the periodic turmoil ever since the well-intentioned expansion proposed by the Robbins' Committee in 1963?

Judged by the £3·5 billion lavished on free tuition and student maintenance, unmatched in Europe and North America, you might expect that all would be very well thank you in the pampered groves of academe. But what do we find?

Free Port?

First take those grand swells of the Vice-Chancellor's Committee. They are up in arms against Kenneth Baker's great education reform bill.

They say he is going too far in controlling how they spend the massive grants to be disbursed by the University Funding Council (which replaces the UGC). They fear a future government could impose conditions that would breach prized academic freedoms. It is a real danger. But shouldn't clever people like VC's understand there's no such thing as free port?

Then there is perennial student lobbying for higher maintenance grants, currently around £2,000 a year. Many get less under the

77

parental means test and complain that their parents fail to make up the difference. It seems a fair complaint. Yet parents have a point against a second means test (on top of assessment for income tax) to finance 'children' up to the age of 25.

Nor are the staff exactly overflowing with gratitude for their comfortable jobs, long holidays, and life tenure (even for the most incompetent), crowned with indexed pensions. Yet when they are not demanding more salaries and perks, they are agitating for more 'research' funds and can turn nasty by denying the PM an honorary degree.

Then what about most taxpayers who never went to universities and earn much less than graduates? Where's the justice in making poorer people who start work at 16 or 18 pay higher taxes to finance more favoured or fortunate students in acquiring a passport to higher lifetime earnings.

If this catalogue of grievances were not enough to establish the Hutber-Harris Law, I have another objection that struck us both as among the founders of the independent University of Buckingham.

To avoid any suspicion of sour grapes, let me first report that since its formal opening in 1976, it has been plagued by none of the tears and tensions that have dogged the state universities. Instead, it has attracted a growing number of satisfied, mostly more mature, students by offering choices denied by the 'free' state sector. These include more broadly-based courses, an intensive two-year degree and more emphasis on personal tuition.

In short, Buckingham has been forced to compete for students by providing distinctive facilities that meet market demand for at least some students better than what's on offer without charge elsewhere.

Perhaps the least obvious objection to state-financed universities is not only that they lack the market incentive to cater efficiently for changing demand. Even worse, by the unfair competition of 'free' provision, they inhibit the vigorous growth of the more varied universities which have to charge students fees to cover tuition costs.

The overriding question is how many more Buckinghams, offering different options, might we have had if the state subsidy were paid direct to students who then paid it to the university of their choice? It's a basic economic rule that if there are to be subsidies, they are best paid to consumers, not handed over to producers who are then free to please themselves rather than their non-paying customers.

Back to Independence

The second question is why don't we restore independence to all universities by moving to student loans which other countries, including socialist Sweden, find acceptable?

There is talk of a piffling Government scheme to lend students up to a total of £1,000 in return for a paltry cut of £100 a year in their maintenance grant. This feeble compromise would predictably stir the beneficiaries of higher learning into the higher decibels without giving them (or the rest of us) anything worth screaming (or cheering) about.

My proposal would be a loan scheme to cover maintenance generously up to £2,500 a year plus, say, a quarter of the tuition fees (ranging from £2,500 for arts at polytechnics to £8,000 for doctors and vets). Instead of Government capital, let banks put up the money and the Treasury provide a guarantee only in the last resort.

Students could then not only choose whether to study away from home, but could pick the course that offered the best value for money. Universities would compete to attract paying customers and receive the balance of three-quarters of fees for every student that chose them.

Sceptics might ponder this quotation:

'The whole system of student awards is thoroughly unfair ... There is no point in tinkering: it should be swept away and replaced by a radical new approach in which student loans play a central part.'

The author? Not Ghengis Tebbit, but that darling of the Left, Tessa (now Lady) Blackstone. We radicals are attracting some surprising allies.

21
A truce between the goodies and baddies

The Sunday Telegraph, 8 May 1988

I FORGET who said that when he heard politicians lay claim to 'compassion' he reached for his gun. In the mouths of party men, especially out of office, compassion usually amounts to the indiscriminate bidding for votes with other people's money.

Before the more biblical word 'charity' was driven out of fashion by the class warriors, we applauded *personal* giving of money or time to self-chosen good causes, with love and without self-advertisement. *Collective* compassion is a fraud because it always depends upon the coercion of taxation. What moral merit is there in making other people do good — if good it be — at gun-point?

The trouble with our modern 'do-gooders' is that they may mean well — apart from those party men who first and foremost are out to do well — but good intentions don't guarantee good results. There is so much evidence to the contrary that I hardly know where to begin.

Moral Outrage

My favourite example is rent control introduced back in 1915 to prevent landlords exploiting possible war-time shortages by pushing up rents. What a perfectly splendid wheeze, say the 'do-gooders' in unison. Yet the malignant results of destroying the market for rented homes have been to imprison people in areas of high unemployment and condemn hundreds of thousands of others to homelessness, squalor, or bed and breakfast hostels.

Another example is foreign aid. What could be more 'compassionate' than for rich countries to send thousands of millions of pounds to governments of poor countries in Africa? It's not only bishops whose breasts are suffused with warm feelings by speeches calling for another billion or two of taxpayers' money on so good a cause.

Yet after decades of 'aid', good intentions have been mocked by widespread poverty, aggravated hunger, centralised power, civil unrest and the piling up of massive debts — which are then blamed on the creditors. If 'do-gooders' were paid by results, they would mostly be reduced to begging benefits for themselves.

Pray understand, my argument is not simply an economist's plea that government social policy is an inefficient way to improve the lot of the poorer people. It is not even that such well-intended collective action may do incidental harm. The case for the prosecution is that conventional 'do-gooders' often turn out, unwittingly, to be evil-doers on a rather grand scale.

Listening to the unending debates on the community charge, the NHS, the social security reforms, I believe the most urgent requirement for our democracy, no less than our economy, is to redress the balance of moral outrage which parodies serious debate as a battle between the goodies and the baddies.

Instead of joining in name-calling against the forces of darkness, I recommend a dose of dispassionate reflection. I start from a dictum of Gilbert Ponsonby, one of the noblest Christian economists I ever knew and an LSE man to boot. He used to say that our approach to social policy should be 'inspired by love, but guided by reason'. In short, good intentions are never enough. We must try to understand the often subtle linkages between cause and effect in economics, as in the natural sciences.

The worst failures in post-war social policy are the result of neglecting a central distinction economists make between the income effect and the incentive effect of all forms of subsidies. To help poor people, the government provides direct cash benefits or lower prices, which include lower rents and 'free' medical care. This has the intended, beneficial result of increasing their effective income so that they can consume more than they could pay for on their own.

At the same time, the subsidy or lower price operates as an unintended incentive to increase demand. A less obvious example from rent control is that protected tenants whose children have left home stay on in a larger house than they need, whilst growing families are doomed to live in a single room. With foreign aid, subsidies to poor countries increase the incentive for client governments to plead poverty.

Dependency Culture

With social benefits the incentive effects lead to even more perverse results. The more generously we raise unconditional benefits for the unemployed, the weaker the inducement for many recipients to work 40 hours a week for net take-home pay that is little, if any, above the value of benefits. Worst of all for my money is the multiplication of that new category of around a million 'single parent families', encouraged by the incentive of special benefits and priority housing.

The intention was no doubt generous, as with help for widows. Who can bear that illegitimate children or victims of broken marriages should suffer from the sins or failings of their parents? Yet immediate relief aimed at *existing* offspring cannot avoid creating a long-term incentive for *continued* irresponsible multiplication of children denied the blessings of family life. In effect, we offer prizes for behaviour most of us would not wish to encourage.

The logic of this neglected analysis is extremely uncomfortable for the majority on all sides of the present debate who care equally about true poverty. It is no good boasting compassion. The more generously we try to relieve hardship *for the able-bodied*, the more we tip the balance of incentives towards widening and deepening dependence on social benefits and against helping people wherever possible to help themselves.

We need a truce while we think how to do better in future. We are unlikely to silence party men seeking votes. But may we not expect more from bishops and others seeking the best long-term interests of their fellows?

22

Now who's blowing smoke in your eyes?

The Sunday Telegraph, 19 June 1988

THE absurd case of the American tobacco company having to pay $400,000 damages to a husband because his wife allegedly smoked herself to death should not cause too much rejoicing even in the ranks of Tuscany.

It is not only as a life-long pipe-smoker that I judge the tobacco abolitionists to be a more lethal threat to the sum of human welfare than the worst smoking can do to any of us. Like all single-issue pressure groups the anti-smoking lobby wildly exaggerates the benefits of its cause and ignores its costs. On tobacco there are several grounds for resisting the propaganda of Action on Smoking and Health (Ash).

First, we should be sceptical of all fashionable fads and fancies about what is good and bad for health. Milk was once so good for children that it was subsidised in schools — until we were warned against dairy produce as a cause of obesity. No less an authority than the government's Egg Marketing Board used to urge us to 'go to work on an egg' — until we learned that we might instead be heading for hospital. Am I now to sue my grocer for giving me too much cholesterol?

No doubt fruit and vegetables will continue to be judged good for most of us, though whether to the exclusion of meat and fish is less certain. But if you develop an allergy to bananas, should you have an action against your greengrocer?

More Doubts

The second doubt is about the 'proof' of a general link between smoking and cancer. The most impressive case for scepticism I have read is in a symposium on *Smoking and Society*.* It includes a review of the 'scientific' evidence by the internationally-famed pyschologist, Professor Hans Eysenck, with a list of references running to 17 pages.

He concludes that the conventional view is unproven and suggests as equally likely that people with a constitutional predisposition to such diseases as lung cancer and coronary heart disease may also have a predisposition to smoke. It seems we have to die of something.

The third doubt about the anti-smokers' case rests on an article in a medical journal which suggested that doctors who gave up the weed were more likely to fall victims to various stress diseases. Some even took to drugs and drinking. We all know of people who stop smoking and put on weight, with obvious costs to their health, to say nothing of their clothes bill.

Even more doubtful is the latest twist in the propaganda about the effect of my smoking on your health, so-called 'passive smoking'. In the symposium quoted above, an American Professor of Pharmacology, Dr Ariado, studies seven pages of 'scientific' references before concluding that the evidence does not support the charge.

But the case against the anti-smoking fanatics goes much wider than making propaganda on the basis of claims that are, in the words of the editor of *Smoking and Society*, 'either wrong, unproven, built upon faulty analysis, or pushed well beyond the point of common sense'.

The more weighty charge is that abolitionists are symptomatic of a naïve, paternalist, authoritarian view that increasingly threatens individual freedom and responsibility throughout Western society. The glory of a market economy is that it gives the widest scope for adults to lead their own lives and, ultimately, to choose the risks they will run.

Where would we be if we had to approve of other people's preferences — and they of ours? The freedom of every individual's choice should be upheld so long as it does not interfere with the exercise of like freedom by others. Purists might say their freedom to avoid contact with tobacco smoke is violated by my smoking. But what of my objection to their indulgence in damaging cosmetics, shocking garbs, frightening hair styles, distracting aftershave, danger-ous sunbathing, risky barbecues, deafening pop music, to say nothing

*Lexington Books, 1986.

of such offensive habits as eating garlic, chewing gum, whistling, and for that matter laughing too loudly — to which I occasionally plead guilty?

The truth is that a free society depends absolutely on the widest degree of tolerance that our self-appointed guardians of taste would reserve only for themselves. Anti-smokers should beware of a pressure group to suppress other people's personal preferences, lest the same bullying technique is deployed against their minority obsessions like skiing, hunting, fishing, pot-holing, jogging, rugby, boxing, flying, horse racing or any activity that others may judge dangerous or undesirable.

Beware

But I have left to the last the most lethal danger which the American legal decision aims at the heart of a free society. Economists defend consumer sovereignty so long as goods and services are offered for sale on the basis of accurate descriptions, wherever appropriate, of their performance or ingredients. For the rest, the rule is *caveat emptor* or, for those of us who didn't go to Oxford, let the buyer beware.

The hidden peril of well-intentioned 'consumer protection' laws is that they lead innocent shoppers to lower their guard instead of keeping their wits about them in buying unproven or unbranded goods. Above all, they should be wary of high-pressure salesmanship. Free choice is a prized right which in turn demands that customers accept responsibility for their buying decisions.

The worst absurdity of the case against the American tobacco company is that its cigarettes carried a health warning. I'm offering a gift of cigarettes, tobacco or cigars for the best suggestion of a comparable warning to pin on these priggish enemies of consumer choice. My first shot is: 'Anti-smokers may damage their own freedom.'

23
Thoughts on buying an old school tie

The Sunday Telegraph, 3 July 1988

CONSIDERING that I left the Tottenham Grammar School in 1943, you may think it a bit late to have only now acquired an old school tie. But the circumstances are rather special.

Although my school dated back to Elizabeth I, if not to Edward VI, it was never as distinguished as such famous foundations as Birmingham and Manchester. Yet it provided generations of boys from poor or modest families in north London with a springboard into industry, the professions and, increasingly in my time, into universities.

I never got caught up with the Old Boys' Association, and feared the worst when it went comprehensive and was re-named Somerset School after our revered benefactress, Sarah, Duchess of Somerset.

Why then did I find myself back at the school last month, queuing-up to buy an old boy's tie? The occasion was a dinner to mark the closure of the school by Haringey council under Bernie Grant. The advertised reason was the continuing fall in numbers of children of school age.

Reasons of Sex

On closer inquiry I gather the number of children attending Tottenham and other Haringey schools has declined faster than elsewhere since Mr Grant and his friends took over. Could it be that Labour is bad for births or good for child mortality?

No, the explanation is that an increasing number of parents are smuggling their offspring across the borders to schools under less malignant régimes like Barnet and Enfield. But why close my old school which remains as strikingly handsome as the day I moved into it, newly-built, in 1940? Surely there are plenty of buildings more fit for demolition?

Maybe, but this school had a far worse defect in the jaundiced eyes of its political masters. As a boys' school, it defiled the pure doctine of universal, undifferentiated, homogenised comprehensive education.

I found myself reflecting how differently this tale — and so much else — might have turned out had it not been for R. A. Butler. It was 'Rab', once my hero, who I now see fatally weakened the British educational system with his acclaimed 1944 Act which abolished fee-paying in state schools. According to left-wing humbug, those of us who got to grammar school as scholarship boys were psychologically scarred for life by being segregated as 'goats' from the fee-paying 'sheep'.

Of course, Butler and the other fashionable education dandies, including most Tories and the middle-class Labour intellectuals, were then public school men. Their fancy, fee-paying schools were left intact. It was only the peasants who could not be expected to pay towards the education of their children!

Yet suppose my old school had retained a fee-paying element? The Institute of Economic Affairs would not have had to launch the idea of an education voucher. With spreading post-war prosperity, more parents could have afforded full or partial fees, especially if the taxes they paid for 'free' education had been reduced. The scholarship element would have declined to the dwindling minority who could not afford to pay. Voters would have learned that a good education was worth buying before a holiday in foreign parts. And then ...? A number of advantages would have followed.

The present generation of children would have been rescued from the grip of the educational faddists. Parents could have voted between schools that were comprehensive, grammar, traditional, modern, single sex or mixed, just as they already vote between supermarkets, corner shops and delicatessens, simply by switching their spending power.

And as in other competitive markets, schools governors would have to cater directly for parental demand. There would be less talk about scruffy, incompetent teachers and more evidence of school uniforms and discipline. And my old school would now be closing down only if it had failed to justify the fees it was charging.

Indeed, if we are to judge by the products of today's flourishing public schools, many of whom are the offspring of self-sacrificing, state-educated parents, there would have been even greater prizes. Not only would there be less educational failure, but less truancy, hooliganism and political contention.

Fitted for Crime

Above all, I venture to assert that in a world where most parents had power to insist on value for the money they spent directly on their children's education, fewer school leavers at 16 or 18 would turn out fitted for little better than unemployment, soccer violence or crime.

Nationalised schools have failed us for the same mixture of reasons as council housing, the NHS and other state monopolies in transport, energy, shipbuilding and motor cars. All end up the playthings of party politics. All yield far too much sway to trade unions and other producer pressure groups. All lack the competitive life force that makes even humdrum managers more efficient. All turn out poor products. Yet all can nevertheless survive for ever on taxpayers' subsidies without heeding the wishes of taxpayers as parents, patients, tenants and customers.

A possible consolation is that the school foundation is likely to finish up with a site worth several million pounds which would be enough to restore the old Tottenham Grammar School with a mixture of fee-payers and scholarship boys. So can we turn the tables on the ghost of Butskellism, put our grandchildren's names down for future places, and wave our old school ties at the impotent local miseducation authority?

Alas, the unenterprising foundation governors appear to have thrown in their lot with local councillors to use the money for the wider 'benefit' of politically dominated 'education' in Haringey. Sarah, Duchess of Somerset, must be spinning in her grave.

24

Socialism a mistake — official

The Sunday Telegraph, 20 November 1988

RECENT dazzling, crisp sunny Sundays in the run-up to Christmas should provoke greater awe at the infinite wonder of God's creation, of which it would be refreshing to hear more from the bishops!

But when did you last ponder the miracle of the economic order? How does it come about that millions of shopping baskets are daily filled with our distinctive choices from thousands of products grown, prepared, packed and transported by anonymous people from distant lands of which we know nothing?

In our working lives most of us contribute towards one link in the chain of invention, production, and distribution leading we often know not where. We are like puppets dancing on strings pulled by wholesalers, retailers and consumers scattered around the country, if not the world.

But why don't the strings get hopelessly tangled? How does it all fit together? Is anyone in charge? Could Bryan Gould's industrial strategy provide an adequate substitute?

The questions multiply. Can anyone know the full ramifications of what is glibly called the 'world economy'? Could the present system ever have been invented by a single mind, or be redesigned by a committee of Nobel laureates? Do we even understand how it came about?

'The Fatal Conceit'

Having devoted most of his 89 years and dozens of publications to puzzling over these questions, the greatest economic and political philosopher of this century, Friedrich Hayek, has now written what may prove his crowning work. It is a brilliant effort to illuminate such mysteries. His title, *The Fatal Conceit*, is a challenge to the ruling intellectual élites of rationalists, empiricists, positivists, utilitarians and other assorted collectivists who think they know it all. Lacking humility, they scorn the spontaneous evolution of what Hayek calls 'the extended order' in which — without human design or central co-ordination — we find:

> 'thousands of millions of people working in a constantly changing environment, providing means of subsistence for others who are mostly unknown to them, and at the same time finding satisfied their own expectations that they will themselves receive goods and services produced by equally unknown people'.

The secret weapon that produces coherence from the apparent chaos of individual striving is, of course, our old friend the market. It appears a simple, even mundane, concept of people shopping around for everyday goods and services. But its ramifications are of wondrous import.

It is markets that make possible an international division of labour which has mocked the Malthusian and Marxist fears of increasing poverty to enable multiplying millions to live at ever-rising standards of living.

It is markets that enable more of whatever people want to be extracted from available scarce resources. The central fact that makes markets more efficient than planning is that relevant knowledge about the possibilities of production, resources, wants, transport and all other variables is widely dispersed. It is certainly not 'given data' as economic theory supposes. Nor is it constant, but ceaselessly shifting with every change in invention, innovation, exploration, individual preferences.

The true miracle of the market is that it takes into account more information than could ever be assembled by the most competent team of central planners, let alone by Lady Blackstone's Institute of Public Policy Research!

'This Marvellous Market'

So what does this marvellous market do? It brings all the scattered, changing information into the reckoning and effortlessly computes and re-computes relative prices as signals which guide equally scattered entrepreneurs, managers, investors, borrowers, dealers and consumers how best to achieve their individual purposes.

If adaptation to changing circumstances is not perfect, a major reason is government intervention to fix prices, protect producers, subsidise declining industries and in a host of other ways to restrict competition and thereby obstruct its pathfinding rôle as the 'optimum discovery procedure'.

Superficial critics object to the idea of buying in the cheapest market and selling in the dearest. To the critics' cry of selfishness or profiteering we may observe that, so long as competition is not suppressed, the effort to maximise profits compels producers to offer customers better price, quality or service. In the market over the long run you have to do good to do well.

Perhaps the most absorbing revelations in Hayek's riveting book are the chapters exploring how the extended order depends on individual property, contract, trade, honesty, law, peaceful striving and saving; and how it evolved from narrow, self-contained, warring, communal, hunting groups in primitive times.

He shows how this evolution required our forebears to subdue the instincts of collectivist solidarity and altruism that were essential to small groups but would have frustrated the morals appropriate to an impersonal market order.

Primitive man sought the obvious visible targets of food and shelter. Today most of us can hardly grasp ultimate ends which our daily labour serves. But this is difficult stuff and must be read in the original by highbrows with the necessary combination of patience, perseverance and sufficient humility to suspend initial disbelief.

Challenging Conclusion

I return to the introductory chapter for Hayek's most challenging conclusion. It is headed: 'Was Socialism a Mistake?' His answer is an unqualified 'yes' and I am now convinced that he is right. The charge against the collectivists of every stripe is that they are wrong about the *facts*.

Their argument is founded on the delusion that the strategic guidance system of market prices can be replaced by what they would call 'rational' commands by some super group of central planners.

They believe they could assemble enough facts to redirect human efforts and to redesign the structure of incentives in conformity with some model of 'social justice'. In place of Adam Smith's 'invisible hand' of competitive markets, socialists would find themselves steering blind what I have called a hand and mouth-operated economy resting on coercion and exhortation.

Where has socialism ever worked to raise standards of living and civilisation? After high hopes, it has failed repeatedly in Russia, China, Poland, Yugoslavia, Vietnam, Tanzania and Nicaragua, despite help from the West in both copying and credits. Who can dismiss Hayek's magisterial verdict: 'To follow socialist morality would destroy much of present human kind and impoverish much of the rest.'

25

Let's privatise sterling next?

The Sunday Telegraph, 4 December 1988

DESPITE the Conservatives' better record on inflation since 1979, renewed anxieties about rising prices pose a fundamental question which came to the fore in the 1970s when Labour presided over inflation rates of between 10 and 25 per cent.

The question is whether money is too important to be left to party politicians. Of course, all governments pay lip service to stable prices. But when faced with awkward choices of policy, can we really expect them to stick to the straight and narrow path of financial rectitude?

It was all so much easier in the days of the gold standard. Not only was the pound sterling tied to a specified weight of gold; the Bank of England was a private company not subservient to spendthrift politicians. True, it had an effective monopoly over the issue of notes, but any temptation to print too many was checked by its liability to give gold in exchange for unwanted currency.

The importance of this discipline was vividly demonstrated during the Napoleonic war when the government suspended convertibility and borrowed heavily from the Bank. Inevitably, the increased supply of paper money forced up prices and the mischief was not checked until gold payments were restored.

Glory of the Gold Standard

In its full glory the gold standard was a self-correcting market mechanism. If prices rose, and people feared for the future value of their savings, they could simply demand gold in exchange for their notes at a fixed rate. The consequent squeeze on the Bank's gold reserve compelled it to contract the supply of notes in circulation, which reduced prices and restored their value.

93

Since 1931 the pound has lost this anchorage in real value and in 1946 the Bank of England was nationalised. As a result, it is no longer scrupulous bankers but the government of the day that determines the quantity of cash and so the size of the inverted pyramid of bank money built up by traditional ratios on that cash base.

The baneful result of trusting politicians with our money is crudely exposed by a chart I have hanging in my office. It shows a rise in the average prices of standard commodities amounting to 30,000 per cent over the seven centuries from 1280 to 1980. Of this 300-fold debasement in our coinage, more than 95 per cent has occurred since the 1930s, and most of that since the last war!

Keynesian Age of Inflation

This great age of inflation has been blamed on the followers of Keynes who, after his death in 1946, went further than him in preaching the expansion of monetary demand as the magic path to perpetual full employment.

To politicians it sounded like a free lunch. They could pursue their favourite pastime of spending more money and have economic growth thrown in as a bonus. Alas, with the help of predatory trade unions, an increasing part of the additional demand was diverted from raising employment and output into boosting incomes and prices.

It was the achievement of Milton Friedman in the 1970s to remind us of the old quantity theory which warned earlier generations that if you increase spending faster than production you are most likely to buy more inflation. His solution seemed simplicity itself. If governments were limited to increasing the money supply by around 2 or 3 per cent a year, it would match the average rate of increased output and so keep prices stable.

But how could party politicians be held to such a strict monetary rule? A number of suggestions were forthcoming in the 1960s. One wicked idea was that Ministerial, Parliamentary and Treasury salaries should be inversely related to prices!

More seriously, Peter Jay suggested that the management of monetary policy should be taken away from such scalliwags and entrusted to a group of independent wise men appointed for long terms and paid well to maintain stable prices. Others went further in suggesting that the Bank of England should be denationalised to remove it from interference by short-sighted, opportunistic politicians.

'Entrenched Legal Limits'

Professor J. M. Buchanan, who recently won wider fame outside America as the leader of the 'public choice' school and a Nobel Laureate, so despairs of democratic governments resisting the temptation to inflate that he now recommends entrenched legal limits on the discretion of politicians to tamper with monetary policy. But what of countries that don't have written constitutions to check the power of temporary majorities?

It was left to the master of them all, F. A. Hayek, to go to the root of the trouble. In 1976, before 'privatisation' had been heard of, he published a Hobart Paper with the remarkable title: *Denationalisation of Money*. His analysis was original yet irresistible. Its essence was that the mismanagement of money is no more than a special case of the abuse of monopoly power. At once the solution suggested itself.

Thus by long usage, reinforced by laws on legal tender, modern governments can require citizens to accept and use the national unit of money, however variable its value. Accordingly, politicians have little incentive to persevere through thick and thin in maintaining honest money. But if people could choose between a number of currencies, the managers of each would have a powerful inducement to check over-issue and preserve its value.

New Monetary Units

The first steps for Hayek were the abolition of exchange control and legal tender laws so that Britons could choose to make contracts in Deutschemarks or Swiss francs, which have proved a better store of value than pounds sterling. It would also be open for banks to launch new monetary units and win customers by doing even better.

Not to be outdone, a young economist named Kevin Dowd has now trumped Hayek in the latest Hobart Paper, entitled *Private Money*. He would go all the way by abolishing the Bank of England and welcoming new brands of pounds tied to the value of specified commodities. It may all seem remote, but so was the abolition of exchange control recommended by yet another Hobart Paper in 1979.

So the Chancellor had better live up to his earlier promise of getting inflation down to zero. Otherwise, more of us will look for a better hole for our savings. But, please, no more talk about a single European currency run by a bunch of super-monopolists fighting over the money supply in a dozen different languages.

26

Hiding behind
Mrs Thatcher's skirt

The Sunday Telegraph, 16 April 1989

SINCE Mrs Thatcher let Jacques Delors's European cat out of the Brussels bag in her Bruges speech last September, debate on the transition from Common Market to Single Market has certainly warmed up. And the more the Bruges text is studied, the less it is seen to deserve the instant outrage of professional Euro-cheer leaders.

Sir John Hoskyns was not the first to comment on the sensitivity of many European spokesmen to any breath of criticism. It would be easy to say too many of them are making too good a living on the Brussels gravy train. But a kinder explanation was offered in the *New European* quarterly by Christopher Tugendhat whose *communautaire* credentials are not inferior to Ted Heath's. He reminds us that the Common Market was conceived after the war by leaders of countries that had been invaded and occupied, if not all defeated. No wonder that outside Britain the concepts of nationality and the nation state were widely discredited.

Hence the dream of federalism, which has survived even after memories of war faded and the nation state reasserted its claims as the primary focus for loyalty and obedience. Now will you insensitive British see why Mrs Thatcher can be pilloried as nationalistic, or at least insufficiently European? Tugendhat patiently explains that all governments believe in *Europe des Patries,* but

> 'the *federal dream* is still alive . . . and is held in respect by many who do not in practice subscribe to it. For that reason attacks upon it are widely and deeply resented'.

Got it?

Earnest Eurocrats

When the British are most often accused of hypocrisy, it's a bit rich to be lectured by earnest Eurocrats for not joining in their silly make-believe about early progress towards political integration, if not a United States of Europe. Such political posturing is especially infuriating because it diverts attention from what Tugendhat agrees is 'the real question', namely, the extent and forms of government intervention within our national economies. This is the issue we should be studying and debating. Just because M Delors believes in more socialist policies than Mrs Thatcher, he can hardly claim to be more European — any more than socialist Neil Kinnock could claim to be more British than non-socialist David Owen.

Tugendhat's illuminating amateur psycho-analysis of our European friends provides a further explanation of why Mrs Thatcher appears more isolated than she really is. Thus there are plenty of French, German, Italian and other European political leaders who privately share her non-socialist views. But lacking her courage, they prefer to join in the well-established game described by a French observer as *se cacher derrière la jupe de Madame Thatcher*. They can hide behind her skirt and keep quiet, confident in the knowledge that in the last resort she will use the veto (wherever it is still effective) to prevent worker participation and all the other socialist mischief of M. Delors's 'social dimension'.

What remains true is that the programme for removing obstacles to trade, investment and migration throughout the Community by 1992, does not require a common statute for companies, or the right of trade unionists to sit on their boards, or to enjoy equal access to social benefits, let alone uniform or minimum wages or conditions of work.

What 1992 does require is the rooting out of all the remaining national restrictions on the freedom of entrepreneurs, employees and consumers to earn their living and spend their income on terms equally available to citizens in all member states.

Gains from Trade

The gains from free trade will be widely shared. Open access will enable all of us to enjoy what was once thought the enriching prerogative of the powerful, to buy in the cheapest market and sell our labour or output in the dearest. Of course, at the start, labour is cheaper in Spain, Portugal or Greece than in Germany, France, or Belgium; just as labour was once dirt cheap in Hong Kong, Singapore — and Japan! But for how long?

Economic theory and recent experience confirm that international trade operates to raise the standards of the poorer and less productive people and regions. In a free market cheap and abundant labour will attract employers, just as high wages elsewhere will attract employees from lower wage areas. Trade depends on geographical difference in costs and other circumstances and the resulting competition tends to equalise prices, incomes and opportunities.

The folly of the so-called 'social dimension' is that M Delors would like to *start* by equalising or 'harmonising' conditions between areas of high and low labour or tax costs to prevent 'social dumping'. Yet if Greek or Portugese employers were saddled at once with paying higher wages and social benefits, the resulting unemployment would be used to justify increased regional subsidies.

In the latest CPS tract, *Europe 1992: The Good and the Bad,* John Redwood MP describes the result as a 'gigantic merry-go-round raising costs, raising taxes and raising subsidies throughout the Community'. As it is, he points out our bill from Brussels will more than double from under £1,000 million last year to close on £2,000 million this year.

Plenty of other voices are at last being raised against the already excessive power of the Commission. They include well-merited attacks on its protectionist proclivities from the Adam Smith Institute in *Bricks in the Wall* and from Professor Brian Hindley in *The World Economy* showing that anti-dumping duties are manipulated to block legitimate competition from lower cost Far Eastern producers — where wages, incidentally, have risen from the pre-war bowl of rice to approaching European levels. Even more fiercely, the radical No Turning Back Group of MPs are shortly weighing in with *Europe: Dream or Nightmare.*

The Promise of 1992

Yet all these critics strongly support the 1992 prospectus which does not include Jacques Delors's fevered socialist hopes for a *dirigiste*

Europe. As explained in the recent classic IEA Paper by Professor Victoria Curzon Price,* 1992 simply promises the removal of impediments to the free movement of goods, services, people and money. Within a single market, differing national social policies, company structures and tax régimes can compete. In this way we will better learn what serves our changing need than by heeding the backward-looking, pre-Gorbachev nostalgia of Master Jacques.

Sir John Hoskyns may or may not be correct in his measured judgement that the Commission lacks the managerial competence to deliver 1992 on time. Certainly it is an ambitious programme with glittering prizes and prospects for all who count themselves European. In the hope that the dreamers and *dirigistes* will not desist, I hereby reveal the new slogan for our Bruges Group.

A boarding party is flying into Bruges next Friday to join other European allies in opening up a second front against M. Delors. On our banner will fly the simple advice *1992 First.* If only he were a fellow cockney, I'd add: 'Come orf it Jack!'.

---

* *1992: Europe's Last Chance? From Common Market to Single Market,* 19th Wincott Memorial Lecture, IEA Occasional Paper 81, London: Institute of Economic Affairs, December 1988. – ED.

27

After ten years her work is not yet complete

The Independent, 31 March 1990

THE reasons for Margaret Thatcher's towering ascendancy — spreading far beyond Britain, as I have discovered in recent visits to Australia, New Zealand, the United States and Russia — will be debated well beyond the 1990s. Her lasting impact on policy around the world is unlikely to be disputed, especially if we take seriously the deathbed conversion of the British Labour Party and the East European ex-Marxists to 'market socialism'.

At every stage, Mrs Thatcher was assailed for wanton confrontation, even conscious cruelty. Every day her resolution was tested. Her unique, indispensable contribution has been the combination of calm, consistent clarity of thought with a personal moral courage that has not been matched by a British politician since Churchill as war-time leader.

The puzzle remains, from where did her transformation of political thinking and policy come? Keynes argued in 1936 that radical changes in the political agenda, such as he was seeking to achieve, stemmed from intellectual influences. He claimed, hopefully, that 'the world is ruled by little else [than] the ideas of economists and political philosophers'. I doubt if Mrs Thatcher would think of herself as an intellectual, though like her political mentor Keith (now Lord) Joseph she enjoys the company of intellectuals, and has even been seen to fall silent in the company of Milton Friedman or Friedrich Hayek. Certainly, a new idea has never entered her head, not in the seminal sense implied by Keynes.

'Thatcherism'

'Thatcherism' is no novel, far less alien, creed. Its central belief in the general benevolence of free market forces operating in a framework of strong but limited government is little more than a return to the broadly shared assumptions of Liberal and Tory leaders during Britain's last great eruption of economic change in the 19th century. If Mrs Thatcher owes a large debt to ideas, they were not her own. Her initial contribution was to be receptive to the seminal, scholarly thinking stemming from Adam Smith and David Hume, as refined in our own times by such Nobel Laureates as Friedrich Hayek, Milton Friedman, George Stigler and James Buchanan.

If the importance of competitive markets, consumer choice, incentives, property rights, stable money and the rest, had been understood for a century or two, wherein lies the lady's claim to fame? As the historians ponder this central riddle, they might start with A. V. Dicey's *Law and Public Opinion in England*. In 1905 he reviewed the progress of legislation since 1800 as a background to what he called 'the growth of collectivism' after 1870. The story was one of multiplying laws, each capable of justification to remedy immediate grievances, but enacted without deep thought about their cumulative, long-term effects. The ruling assumption was 'a belief in the benefit of governmental guidance or interference, even when it greatly limits the sphere of individual choice or liberty'.

'The Mounting Collectivist Consensus'

There followed seven decades of what I call the mounting collectivist-Keynesian-Beveridge-welfare consensus. Encouraged by mobilisation for two world wars and sped-up by Labour governments, policy was guided by the paternalistic, basically anti-democratic sentiment that every economic or social imperfection of a free society justified new laws that diminished the individual action and aggrandised the state. But the philosophers of the market economy predicted that government failure would prove more crippling than market failure.

Politicians not only lack the knowledge to control an increasingly complex, changing economy; their policies are distorted by special interest groups, like trade unions, farmers, welfare and other lobbies. Worst of all, their *ad hoc* interventions wreak havoc in the market-place with disruptive strikes, distortionary inflation, demoralising unemployment, debilitating taxes and the dubious black economy.

The question being asked in the 1970s was whether Britain was any longer governable by the weakened authority of parliamentary democracy. After the debacle of Ted Heath's U-turn, it was Mrs Thatcher's good luck to have her turn at reversing the tables in 1979 when Labour was caught out treating deep-seated union ills with the political poultice of a 'social contract'. After 1979 Mrs Thatcher simply went ahead and governed.

The consensus lauded by the great and the good can now be seen to have been no more than civilised but cowardly appeasement.

'Pricking the Bubble'

All other post-war prime ministers had shrunk back in fear of powerful unions in alliance with the dominant collectivist sentiment that Fabian and Marxist intellectuals have been puffing up over almost a century. Mrs Thatcher alone took courage to prick the bubble.

Her work is far from complete. Ten years is not sufficient to reverse a century of relative decline. When the time comes, her successor will need, first, similar courage to resist the re-grouping of remnants of the old consensus; and second, the same commitment to enlarge individual choice against the Hobson's choice of ever-growing government.

I do not know Michael Heseltine personally, but I'm still looking for evidence that his splendid self-confidence conceals a little modesty about the ability of politicians, here or in Europe, to solve all our problems.

28
High price of a social market

A trendy new label disguises the sacrifice of more and more of our incomes, writes Ralph Harris.

The Sunday Telegraph, 17 February 1991

WHAT are we to make of the recent discovery, by Mr Norman Lamont and Mr Christopher Patten, of the 'social market' as the Conservative watchword for the 1990s and beyond? First, it should be pointed out that the two politicians are not two of a kind. Their past attitudes suggest that Mr Lamont attaches more importance to the market half of the phrase and Mr Patten to the social. Mr Patten's contribution came in a contrived address to the leftish Policy Studies Institute, whose acolytes lap up such a think-piece like the Anglican Synod swallowing yet another revised services sheet.

But was it simply a PR gloss by a hard-pressed party chairman to divert attention from deepening economic gloom? Or was it another semantic effort to distance the Tories from their deposed leader — who kept them in power for more than a decade? Or might it portend a shift towards the middle ground where Neil Kinnock has been driven by the very success of the Thatcherite market economy?

Since Mr Patten is a leader of the wet tendency and currently drafting the next election manifesto, we must try to take his words seriously. So let us ask what exactly is meant by the 'social market economy'.

The most precise answer I can offer is either absolutely nothing — or almost anything. If Mrs Thatcher and her supporters believe in the unadorned 'market economy', does that mean it is unsocial — or anti-social? Are we to understand that Hume, Smith, Robbins, Jewkes,

Hayek, Friedman and other sophisticated champions of the market
were engaged in some plot against society?

Free Markets Are Social Markets

If you wish to be analytical, the reality is that the competitive market is
necessarily a *social* instrument. It is nothing less than a network of
local, national and international links that enable people to trade
together freely for their mutual benefit, as workers, consumers,
producers, dealers, savers, borrowers, investors.

It is the spread of this market that has so wondrously widened
prosperity and extended freedom of choice throughout the West. Because it developed spontaneously (in Hayek's words 'the result of human
action but not of human design'), is it to be stigmatised as unsocial?

The market could be regarded as 'social' in another sense. Thus it
operates within a developing framework of laws, customs, and
standards which extend from approved weights and measures to help
in cash and kind for those who cannot help themselves. Its supporters
differ on the scope for reforming the legal framework. But for true
market men the test is to avoid sapping its efficiency in maximising
valued output or its flexibility in adapting to ceaseless changes in
resources, technology, competition and consumer preferences.

For all the 19th-century jibes against the phantom of *laissez faire*,
there is no such animal as a free market operating in a vacuum of state
inaction. If we stick to precise language, then full-blooded socialists
aside, we all accept some measure of a mixed economy. But as with
whisky and soda, everything turns on the mixture.

In his crowning work, *The Fatal Conceit*, Hayek quotes Confucius:
'When words lose their meaning, people will lose their liberty.' On this
text he hangs a warning against the misuse of the words 'social' and
'society' which too easily imply a common pursuit of shared objectives
wholly hostile to individual freedom. He cites the *Fontana Dictionary of
Modern Thought* with 35 uses of 'social' which come, he thinks
appropriately, after the entry for 'soap opera'!

Weasel Word

Hayek scorns 'social' as a weasel word, which empties the noun it
qualifies of all meaning, just as a weasel is said to empty the contents

of an egg without leaving a trace. He adds that it is 'a semantic fraud from the same stable as "People's Democracy".'

Mr Patten and others have been known to take refuge behind the German adoption of 'social market' to describe their successful post-war economy. Hayek, who knew Ludwig Erhard as a professor, not a politician, quotes him as saying that the market economy did not have to be *made* social since it was already so by its very nature. In any event, the German miracle after 1948 owed everything to curbing the state, unleashing market forces, and learning from past suffering to avoid the plague of inflation.

Should we then dismiss this latest talk about the 'social market' as no more than a verbal flourish or a harmless misunderstanding? I find no grounds for such comfort. Mr Patten's speech went on to hint that his ambition is to lavish more resources on yet another bid to rescue failing state social services from public obloquy. He wants to make them so good that people no longer think it worth paying for private education or medical care. Not much hope, or danger, of that.

But let me ask bluntly in his own terms, why it is more 'social' to go to a state school (as I did) rather than to Eton, or to use an NHS bed rather than subscribing privately (as I do) for a Bupa nursing home? If Mr Patten wants more state (nationalised) welfare, with all the attendant waste and damage to the market, why not say so openly and argue his case on costs, rather than hide behind obfuscations about the 'social market'?

His fuzzy approach was well exposed by Professor Robert Skidelsky, who as Keynes's official biographer understands economics and wrote as impressive tract on *The Social Market Economy* for David Owen's old SDP group. His central principle is that 'we turn to the market as first resort and the government as last resort ... our first instinct is to use the market, not to override it'. His own commitment to the market led him to conclude from endemic congestion in the public sector that rationing by price is both feasible *and necessary* in such services as roads *and hospitals*. He emphasises that without direct payment there is no accountability. No 'social market' nonsense here.

Political Cost of 'Social Market'

I would go further in challenging Mr Patten's version of the 'social market'. His wing of the post-Thatcher Conservative Party have always

106

wanted a larger role for government. Their inspiration is not so much social as self. Thus they are self-conscious intellectuals of the self-confident, not to say self-righteous, school who do not easily defer to ordinary people's preferences expressed through the market. They put more spending before tax cuts, especially if superficial pollsters say there are votes in it. They prefer politicisation to privatisation.

Above all, these new missionaries of the so-called 'social market' have not reckoned on the cost of whetting appetites for more state spending in the run-up to an election. Once politicians relax their guard, there are a thousand lobbies each with plausible claims for a few more millions, or tens of millions.

Even Mrs Thatcher's determination could not hold the line against mounting government spending, which by 1990 was running above 45 per cent of the nation's income. What will satisfy these closet collectivists — 50 or 60 or 70 per cent? Thus does talk of 'social market' raise the spectre of socialist market — just when a growing army of young Thatcherite economists in the East are looking to us for inspiration.

29

Can Britain survive without signing?

The Sunday Telegraph, 8 December 1991

YES. If John Major can summon up the courage of his own convictions, he will pack some throat lozenges and earplugs but no pen or chequebook when he leaves on Monday for Maastricht. There's more talking than listening for him to do but absolutely no need to sign anything, least of all damaging and expensive commitments.

The Prime Minister neither wants nor needs anything from Maastricht — except, alas, the fig-leaf of an agreement. There is no question of Britain leaving the EC. The question always was how little must we give away this time round, in return for what? For nothing more than a good press in the run-up to the General Election?

But the price we would pay for signing — and therefore *what we stand to gain by not signing* — is much more than the concessions already yielded up, with more to come at the summit in return for dropping that F-word.

First, most of the provisions on political and monetary union would weaken the competitive efficiency of the Single Market and, secondly, would strengthen the remorseless federal, centralising tendencies. Thirdly, even if we keep our opt-out clause and let the rest go ahead with EMU, monetary union would still cost us a pile of Ecus towards the subsidies demanded by Spain and others to offset the damage to their less-developed economies.

Fourthly, the imposition of still more complex conditions of membership would make it more difficult for the liberated countries of Eastern Europe to join up. Finally, if we boldly play our precious veto, we would be keeping our shield against being outvoted again.

Such an outcome would in no way affect our continued participation in the Single Market. In his Commons speech the Prime Minister acknowledged that the 'positive advantages' we gained from Europe all came from participating in 'the world's largest single market'.

By not being stampeded into signing up for political and monetary union, Britain, along with the other 11, remains bound by the existing treaties. We lose none of the present advantages of free movement in goods, services, capital and people promised for 31 December 1992.

And if the others go ahead with political and monetary experiments outside the present treaties and institutions of the basic European Economic Community, they would end up burdening their own economies and handing a welcome competitive advantage for British exports in Europe.

30

A glittering prize in Maastricht's mud

European integration can be achieved
without the folly of federalism.

The Times, 7 June 1993

EVER since Margaret Thatcher spoke at Bruges of the danger of a
European superstate, I have been trying to work out who really wants
to speed up political union rather than consolidating the more widely
supported common market — which is what Edward Heath sold us 20
years ago.

It is easy to see why Jacques Delors and his fellow commissioners
should wish to enlarge still further their powers and prominence. Not
only are they mostly former politicians with a fatal itch to do good, but
several have ambitions to be called home to higher things. As for the
bureaucrats under them, they are sufficiently human to favour
enlarging their empires.

But why do national leaders want to cede further power into these
grasping hands in Brussels? There is no mystery about Spain and the
other mendicant nations whose support has been purchased by
promises of subsidies from the new 'cohesion fund'. But what about
countries that will pay the higher bills?

Two Europes

In his recent paper, *A Tale of Two Europes*, Lord Beloff recalls the
laudable post-war aim of the Treaty of Rome, to construct a Franco-
German axis around which there could be integration of the
continental states 'whose confidence in their own institutions had been
destroyed'. Alas, they also shared many inward-looking, cultural,

110

dirigiste, and legal traditions that remain wholly different from, even hostile to, Britain's international, liberal, Anglo-Saxon roots.

Why then should British leaders tag along — apart of course from John Major and the dwindling band of sycophants who regard Maastricht as Mr Major's personal triumph? Above all, how can this statist progression be supported by Tories, least of all the numerous erstwhile allies of Mrs Thatcher? Part of the answer is that severe whipping dragooned many doubters into the Aye lobby. But what of Geoffrey Howe, David Howell and others who share my understanding and enthusiasm for a liberal market economy?

One clue may be a speech by Geoffrey Howe as Foreign Secretary in 1989 when he described Europe as 'the necessary vehicle, the central fulcrum, the basic lever for Britain to exercise the influence it wishes to exercise in the world'. Such Foreign Office games-playing does not take into account the real world and is doomed to exacerbate national rivalries. Above all, it underestimates the glittering prize of true European integration, without Maastricht, through completing the single market in a liberal framework.

One of Adam Smith's insights was that if all barriers to free trade were ended *'the different states into which a great continent was divided would so far resemble the different provinces of a great empire'.* In short, a genuine common market based on mutual recognition is a benign method of integration; an invisible empire which is the best antidote to the recurrence of war. It was specifically to speed the removal of tariffs, subsidies and other distortions to competition that Mrs Thatcher assented to the Single European Act in 1986. Alas, by ending the national veto, this crucial federalising measure opened the door wider to the subordination of British law to edicts from Brussels, and the imperialism of the European Court in Luxembourg.

Costly Standards of the Superstatists

Ever since, the superstatists have exploited majority voting to impose ruinously costly standards that are not only unnecessary but diametrically opposed to competing jurisdictions implicit in free trade. Where trade depends on differences in national, regional and local production costs, the corporatist pressure from Brussels is for harmonisation and standardisation to suit established interests.

M Delors recently gave the game away by calling for 'a global social charter' to stop competition from the East. This is not a level playing field. It is the ultimate in flat earth economics.

Forget the nonsense about the British sausage, French cheeses, the straight cucumber. Even without Maastricht, remote Eurocrats are forever pushing to impose the 48-hour week, discourage part-time working, ban schoolboy newspaper rounds, censor tobacco advertising, push equal pay to absurd limits, harmonise taxes and more mischief besides. What is all this to do with them, or with the single market? How long before nothing is left for us to decide for ourselves? Poor Mr Major takes refuge in talk about enlarging membership; but how will the less productive economies of Eastern Europe jump these hurdles, which are in truth designed to keep them out?

The case against Maastricht is that it mightily accelerates this intrusive process. It enlarges the so-called 'competence' of the Commission. It extends majority voting in 100 directions. It augments various slush funds and increases taxation. It inflates costs, reduces flexibility and brings fortress Europe nearer. Above all, the obsession with an irreversible monetary union threatens to reduce economic self-government to empty ceremonial. It is a distraction and a detraction from the single market.

'Centralising Logic'

It is simply adding insult to injury for whipped friends of Maastricht to boast of the insertion of 'subsidiarity' and the removal of 'federal' when actions and analysis tell so eloquently of the centralising logic of European political union. By now the emollient Mr Major should have discovered that appeasement — as in 1938 — buys only temporary respite from pressure. Already we read another federal ambush is being prepared when the Belgians take over the presidency next month.

Constitutional scruples aside, the real case for a referendum is that it would buttress the government for the continuing struggle, which I fear would be all the more acrimonious if the sovereign people misguidedly voted Yes.

The End of Macro-Economics?
DAVID SIMPSON

1. The distinguishing feature of developed market economies is incessant qualitative change. New consumer and capital goods, and new methods of production and distribution are continuously being created and old ones destroyed.

2. Macro-economics looks at economic activity in terms of aggregates and averages. It obscures rather than assists an understanding of the essential features of economic activity in a market economy.

3. Macro-economics makes unwarranted assertions about the stability of empirical relationships between aggregates, assumes their unchanging composition, abstracts from essential elements of economic acitivity, and uses concepts out of context.

4. It is impossible to predict to what extent an increase in aggregate demand will be reflected in price rises and to what extent in output increases. In order to know what significance to attach to a numerical value for any aggregate, one has to disaggregate.

5. Aggregate concepts such as the NAIRU, the quantity of money, the output gap and competitiveness are all misleading, and have contributed to the implementation of unsuccessful and sometimes harmful policies.

6. Almost 20 years since it was publicly acknowledged that a government could not spend its way out of a recession, it has been discovered that the fine-tuning of bank lending does not work either. In the UK the operation of monetary policy has been uncoupled from macro-economic theory.

7. The cycle is an intrinsic part of the deregulated developed market economy and one cannot have the benefits of growth without it.

8. Repeated surveys have shown the complete failure of all attempts at short-term forecasting using macro-economic models. Only pattern predictions are possible.

9. Macro-economic theory is a dead-end in the history of economic thought. The way forward is to return to the classical tradition which emphasises the importance of uncertainty, innovation, entrepreneurship and institutional evolution, and has quite different policy implications.

10. Policies to approach full employment must facilitate the adaptation of workers from old jobs to new jobs. Taxes should be shifted from employment to consumption and subsidies should shift from unemployment to the search for, and acceptance of, new employment.

ISBN 0-255 36338-9

Hobart Paper 126

The Institute of Economic Affairs
2 Lord North Street, Westminster
London SW1P 3LB
Telephone: 071-799 3745

£8.00 inc. p.+p.

Regulating Utilities: The Way Forward

There is worldwide interest in Britain's 'experiment' in privatising its principal utilities (gas, electricity, telecommunications, water, railways and airports) and in the system of independent regulation which is designed to curb monopoly power and promote competition.

In this book, the present state of regulation is examined both by leading independent commentators on the subject and by the regulators themselves who discuss the views of the commentators. Fundamental principles are analysed as well as the practical issues involved in regulating each of the six major utilities. Two papers examine general issues — regulating networks and avoiding the abuse of monopoly power.

The book discusses not only the issues which have arisen so far but points the way forward for British utility regulation.

Contents

ISBN 0-255 36337-0   IEA Readings 41

£15.50
inc. p.+p.

The Institute of Economic Affairs
2 Lord North Street, Westminster
London SW1P 3LB
Telephone: 071-799 3745